Dean Verdoe
#24

LeRoy Guaphato
#10

Darrell Kreno
#15

Rob
Dykstra

MW01382655

EDGERTON
A MINNESOTA BASKETBALL LEGEND

EDGERTON
A MINNESOTA BASKETBALL LEGEND

TOM TOMASHEK & KEN KIELTY

Tom Tomashek　　*Ken Kielty*

NORTH STAR PRESS OF ST. CLOUD, INC.
St. Cloud, Minnesota

Copyright © 2008 Tom Tomashek & Ken Kielty

ISBN-13: 978-0-87839-282-7
ISBN-10: 0-87839-282-3

First Edition, November 2008

All rights reserved.

Printed in the United States of America

Published by
North Star Press of St. Cloud, Inc.
P.O. Box 451
St. Cloud, Minnesota 56302

northstarpress.com
info@northstarpress.com

CONTENTS

Acknowledgments vii

Preface ix

Introduction xi

Chapter One	Edgerton, the Early Years	1
Chapter Two	Post Nickerson and Brovold and World War II	22
Chapter Three	The Building Years	40
Chapter Four	A Change in Command	59
Chapter Five	The Regular Season	75
Chapter Six	The District and Regional Tournament	94
Chapter Seven	The Legend Evolves	117
Chapter Eight	The State Tournament	137
Chapter Nine	The Celebration	164
Chapter Ten	The Years After	181

Where Are They Now? 210

Sources 227

Index 229

EDGERTON

Acknowledgments

Edgerton, a Minnesota Basketball Legend was a two-man collaboration that began early in March of 2006. Tom Tomashek did the writing while Ken Kielty, a former Edgerton High School teacher and coach, provided many of the sources, a great deal of background and insight, and worked hand in hand with the publisher.

In the process, more than one hundred interviews were conducted, a half dozen visits were made to Edgerton, and much of the research required hours in history centers and newspaper offices. All this involved the cooperation of countless individuals, far too many to mention all, but we would be remiss not to single out a handful who provided Herculean support.

For starters, we owe a major debt of gratitude to coach Rich Olson, his wife, Marlys, the 1960 Flying Dutchmen players and their families for providing insight and information into what is obviously the book's focus. We must thank Casey DeJong for helping guide us through Edgerton's early years in athletics, Charles Deremo for contributing his handwritten notes of Edgerton High School activities through more than three decades, and former Edgerton High School superintendent Bill Fure for background on the team's tournament run.

Jill Fennema and Irene Gunnick, and the *Edgerton Enterprise* staff were always available when asked to provide photographs, specific dates, and general background, and we couldn't have asked for more assistance than we received from Marilyn Schoolmeester, an Edgerton High School teacher, who spent many hours searching for and duplicating Flying Dutchmen team and individual photos. The hospitality of Ethelyn and Norm Fey and her research.

Finally, we have to acknowledge Barb Kielty and Laura Tomashek, wives who not only were patient during a lengthy project but provided hands-on and spiritual support for more than two years.

PREFACE

The Flying Dutchmen: Minnesota State H.S. Basketball Champs 1959 – 1960

I'm not sure which would have been a better movie: The *Hoosiers* or "The Flying Dutchmen." Yes, *Hoosiers* was a huge success and, surely, a beautiful story about a small town basketball team winning the Indiana State High School Basketball Championship. Well, "The Flying Dutchmen" of Edgerton is the same beautiful story—a different place, Minnesota, a different time, 1960, with different participants.

As the men's basketball coach at Luverne, Minnesota, I was well aware of the great basketball being played in the southwestern part of Minnesota. Edgerton was one of those teams expecting to have another good year. However, no one, I mean no one, would have picked the Edgerton team to represent our region, one of eight regions in the state of Minnesota, let alone win the state championship. Well, possibly one person—that person would have been Ken Kielty, their coach for four years before Richie

Olson took over as a first-year coach. Coach Olson knew he had a veteran team coming back and did all the right things to let them play the game as they knew how.

Winston Churchill once said, "There is nothing more exhilarating than to be shot at and having them miss." Well, I don't think there was anything more exhilarating for fans from Edgerton, and yes, for me, an opposing coach —witnessing their trip to the state tournament as they defeated three strong teams in the state tournament, remaining undefeated, then, watching their glorious escort home to Edgerton.

I liked that team then, and knowing some of those team members now, I can assuredly say, that was not a "miracle team"—it was a team of great players, well coached, and a community that supported its dream.

Coach Bob Erdman
St. James High School (1952) "Hall of Fame," Gustavus (1952-1956) "Hall of Fame," U of M (1957-1958) and Basketball Assistant, plus many summers.

Coached at Mapleton (1956-1957), Luverne (1958-1961), St Cloud Tech (1961-1965), and Alexander Ramsey "Roseville Area Schools" (1965-1996) with a break to coach at Gustavus (1981-1986). Coached both men and women with seven trips to the state tournament.

Member of: Minnesota Basketball Coaches (MBCA) and (MSHSL) "Hall of Fame."

INTRODUCTION

On the night of March 26, 1960, Edgerton Public School won the Minnesota State High School League basketball championship, defeating Austin before a record crowd of 19,018 in Williams Arena.

The Flying Dutchmen, representing a small southwest Minnesota hamlet and led by first-year coach Rich Olson, less than two years removed from Macalester College, completed the season with a 27 and 0 record, highlighted by a nine-game tournament run through District 8, Region II, and three state tournament contests.

In state history of one class, spanning from 1913 through 1970, thirty-one schools won at least one high school basketball title, but no town with a smaller population—certainly not one with two high schools—claimed Minnesota's premier high school championship. Since that enchanted evening in Williams Arena, countless Minnesota athletes have won individual or shared team titles, but most of their names have faded from memory or have been obscured by the proliferation of professional sport, and

EDGERTON

remain archived only in scrapbooks, high school trophy cases, and newspaper microfilm.

Not so for the Edgerton legend, a story of a scrawny bunch of country kids from southwest Minnesota who in three nights vaulted from obscurity to statewide acclaim. Somehow members of the World War II and baby-boomer generations have carried the legend into the twenty-first century, and every March when the state high school basketball tournament rolls around, sportswriters and fans relive the Flying Dutchmen's improbable journey.

Just as improbable as the legendary journey was, is its remarkable durability that begs myriad questions. Why does mention of Edgerton, decades later, still evokes such responses as "Oh, the basketball town"? How is it that, for some, the names of Edgerton starters Veenhof, Verdoes, Kreun, Graphenteen, and Wiarda roll off the tongue as readily as Tinkers to Evers to Chance? Why does 6-foot-7 Gerry Ruda, when it's revealed he was born and raised in Edgerton, still must explain why he played in the Flying Dutchmen band rather than on the basketball team?

The legend follows former Edgerton stars and residents, past and present, sometimes in unlikely places far beyond Minnesota's borders.

In the summer of 1986, Dean Veenhof, Edgerton's two-time all-state center, and his family vacationed in Big Sky Country and one stop was Yellowstone National Park. That day Veenhof's wife, Judy, chose to wear a T-shirt which on the front was inscribed with "Oofta," an endearing Minnesota term. A gentleman asked if she was from Minnesota, and she responded that her family lived in New York, but her husband had been born and raised in a small town in southwest Minnesota. He asked for the town's name. She told him Edgerton. He quickly broke

XII

into a smile and proudly rattled off the five starters' names.

Mention of Edgerton has generated animated conversations in a Michigan church basement, a South Dakota motorcycle rally, a taxi ride in New York City, a stop light in Colorado, stopovers in Florida, Texas, and Arizona senior communities, a New York state athletic seminar, and countless other places.

"Whenever I mention that I'm from Edgerton, I simply just pause and wait for the response," said Judy Roelofs Kreun, high-school sweetheart and now wife of former Flying Dutchmen guard Darrell Kreun.

Sometimes even words were unnecessary in relating the Flying Dutchmen legend. When Edgerton's Jim Van Nieuwenhuyzen was a delivery man for the *Sioux Falls Argus-Leader*, he met a deaf mute who, in hand language, inquired where Van Nieuwenhuyzen lived. Van Nieuwenhuyzen indicated Edgerton, and the man smiled before pumping his hands up and down as if dribbling a basketball.

That the legend continues beyond the championship season is amazing in itself, for 1960 was a watershed year for Minnesota sports, amateur and professional. The 1960 U.S. hockey squad, teeming with Minnesota players, surprised the world by defeating the Soviet Union for Olympic gold. The University of Minnesota Gopher baseball team won its second College World Series in four years. The Golden Gopher football team won the national championship for the first time in nearly twenty years. The NBA Minneapolis Lakers left to become the Los Angeles Lakers. And finally, Minneapolis-St. Paul began its transformation into a national sports market by luring baseball's Washington Senators and convincing the National Football

EDGERTON

League to give it an expansion team the next year. Today, we know those teams as the Twins and Vikings.

Edgerton may not have been the greatest high school team ever to win a Minnesota state title, but the Flying Dutchmen produced one of the state's greatest stories by winning the title at a time when nearly 500 public schools participated in only one classification rather than being split into four sections. Edgerton, population 1,019, became the smallest town ever to produce a state basketball champion, and its Flying Dutchmen's 27 and 0 record made it only the eleventh team in forty-eight years to finish the season undefeated, only the third to do so in post-World War II history.

Never had so few done so much to delight so many in the traditional three March nights in Williams Arena where the Flying Dutchmen defeated Chisholm, Richfield, and Austin—defeating the latter 72 to 61 before a record crowd of 19,018 in the Saturday night championship game. So special was the Flying Dutchmen feat that in *Gopher State Greatness,* a book chronicling Minnesota high school basketball from 1952 through 1981, author Joel B. Krenz opined that Edgerton's legend would endure as long as the game, a prediction time has validated.

"You sort of got a sense at the time that it was going to be a special event," former Flying Dutchmen forward Dean Verdoes says, "but it's created more interest than we ever could have imagined. It certainly was a good feeling to have won, but a better feeling for me is the understanding how it all came together."

Long before Edgerton chartered a public school, the town embraced basketball and supported an adult independent team. The high school, established in the early 1920s, compiled a respectable basketball tradition through the forties, but the team never advanced beyond District 8 and struggled even more when the Christian School, a Dutch reform institution, opened just around the corner and staked claim to a share of the small community's basketball pool.

In 1959, the Flying Dutchmen finished 17 and 5 and reached the District 8 final before losing on a last-second shot to Jasper. The loss was another in a series of heartbreakers for Edgerton, but provided some of the impetus for the coming season. The Flying Dutchmen lost their coach, Ken Kielty, in the off-season but four starters and several promising B team players returned.

New coach Olson, just twenty-three, possessed a profound acumen for the game. He was fiery on the bench, given to shouts of outrage and more than occasionally taunted officials, but he always was in control and adaptable to opposing strategies. He wasn't particularly impressed when he first saw his players but soon discovered their scrawny appearance belied a talent and passion for the game. Pickup basketball always was in season in Edgerton.

"I coached for sixteen years and I was in the [athletic] business for thirty-six years, and I've always said that the hardest thing for a coach is to get a kid to understand his role, and I felt that everyone on that team understood. No one worried about who scored. They didn't turn the ball over," Olson says. "Veenhof, Kreun, and Verdoes were what you might call stars, but if Graphenteen and Wiarda didn't play their roles we didn't win. They also were always steady emotionally, worked hard, and obeyed authority, a reflection of their upbringing in that Dutch reform community. I honestly think that they would have won in any era."

In retrospect, the 1960 Flying Dutchmen provided not only Edgerton but also Minnesota a role model, a group of players who were soft-spoken off the court but hard-nosed in competition and poised in pressure situations. They played the consummate team game with each knowing what to do in Olson's relatively uncomplicated but seamless game plans.

"I thought of them as the ultimate team," *Sioux Falls Argus* sports editor John Egan said. "It just didn't make any difference where the ball went, the guy who had it knew what to do."

On Saturday night, after Edgerton had completed its championship run, Daryl Stevens, who played a tremendous reserve role in the triumph, quickly showered and then climbed to one of the highest points in cavernous Williams Arena. The senior took a seat and focused on the dimly lighted, deserted hardwood court below and experienced a bittersweet moment, warmed by the glowing memories of the season but saddened by the realization that the majestic journey had come to an end.

What Stevens didn't realize was that while every season has an end, the epics are passed from generation to generation. The team from tiny Milan, Indiana, whose 1952 state championship inspired the movie "Hoosiers," had nothing more than a screenwriter over the 1960 Dutchmen legend.

CHAPTER ONE
Edgerton, the Early Years

In 1876, approximately fifteen years before Dr. James Naismith created basketball and posted the game's thirteen rules, A.A. Dodge, M.M. Gunsolus, and A.D. Kingsbury secured 640 acres of Osborne Township, a portion of the sprawling farm country situated between the Chanarmbe River on the east and the Rock River on the west. Not long after the trio's arrival, the town of Edgerton was established by the investors and a handful of settlers lured by the rich farmland and knowledge that the Southern Minnesota Railroad was going to run through the township.

By 1880, according to a federal census, Osborne Township's population was listed at eighty-six, and within the next year the count had more than doubled, many of the newcomers being Dutch coming from Iowa and Illinois. In addition to affordable land, they were enticed by the apparent promise of prosperity and a peaceful way of life. They brought with them an ironclad resolve, a strong work ethic and a Christian faith as solid as the bedrock Sioux quartzite on which the community was built.

Agriculture was the area's industry of choice, with farmers reaping handsome dividends from wheat, rye, flax, oats, potatoes, corn, and some livestock. In the hub of this agricultural Mecca, the community quickly expanded and before 1885 included fifteen businesses, a post office, a railroad station, and a newspaper, the *Edgerton News*. The newspaper failed initially but after a two-and-one-half-year hiatus was resurrected as the *Edgerton Enterprise* and became Pipestone County's newspaper of record.

The addition of grain elevators, mills, and a large storage warehouse would enhance the economic growth. Edgerton was such a thriving community, commercially and socially, that by 1900 it had more than 350 residents, virtually all Christians who belonged to one of the five houses of worship lining Church Street. The churches became the center of social activity, but entertainment also could be found on Main Street and in one of several social lodges, where glee clubs and bands would perform and dances were conducted on special occasions. Temperance and political debates also were not uncommon.

So what, one might ask, did James Naismith have to do with a small farming community in southwestern Minnesota?

The answer probably is not a great deal more than did General Alonzo J. Edgerton, the community's namesake. General Edgerton, a native of Rome, New York, hadn't fought a battle within a hundred miles of the southwestern Minnesota area, but two early settlers—George Dodd and A.D. Kingsbury—who served with Edgerton during the Civil War—persuaded community leaders to name the town after their former leader.

As for Naismith, he developed basketball at Springfield College in Massachusetts and never hung a peach crate closer to Minnesota than the University of Kansas in Lawrence, where he served as the school pastor, a counselor, and basketball coach. Among Naismith's players was Forrest "Phog" Allen whose players included future coaching legends Dean Smith of the University of North Carolina and Adolph Rupp of the University of Kentucky.

Once introduced to basketball, the populace quickly embraced the game that eighty years later established a permanent link between the town and Minnesota sports lore. What made the game so appealing in Edgerton is subject to speculation, but there are several reasonable theories.

Basketball required more finesse than physical force, making it available to both genders. Basketball was an indoor activity that required little space and time and was played primarily in the winter when the farmers and their youngsters were afforded precious downtime. Maybe it had to do with the culture of working together as the area farmers did, particularly during difficult times. When one man was the victim of illness, injury or family emergency, his neighbors worked his fields or tended to his family needs. Through the years, no Pipestone County community was more conscientious than Edgerton when it came to raising funds for worthy causes such as the Sister Kenny Institute, the Red Cross, and later blood drives.

Another possibility is Naismith's own background. Although communications were limited in the era—radio being in its infancy and television not even fantasy—the Edgerton residents with a rigid religious bent might have discovered that basketball's creator also was a minister who graduated from the Presbyterian College of Theology in Montreal in 1890. Naismith was a YMCA education instructor in Springfield, Massachusetts, when he created basketball, an indoor game convenient for students at the School for Christian Workers during the long and cold New England winters. He not only created the game, he did so with a major emphasis on sportsmanship, tolerating neither ruffian behavior nor obscenities.

Based on Sandra Beckering's *Edgerton Minnesota: A History from 1879 to 1979*, and Calla R. Scott's *The History of Edgerton, Minnesota*, sports played a major role in the town's early social calendar. In addition to recreational summer activities, organized town team baseball and league play became popular in the late 1880s with Jess Wroten ostensibly being the first curveball pitcher in Pipestone County. The 1900 Fourth of July celebration was perhaps the most festive occasion in the town's brief history, a societal spectacular featuring brass bands, glee clubs, a parade, a baseball game in which Trosky defeated Edgerton 6 to 3, and a ballyhooed stallion race at the local horse racing dirt oval constructed in 1895.

Minnesota played an integral part in basketball history on February 9, 1895, when the Minnesota State School of Agriculture (now the University of Minnesota) defeated Hamline College 9 to 3 in the nation's first intercollegiate game, and a year later, the host University of Iowa defeated the University of Chicago 15 to 12 in the nation's first college game featuring five-man lineups. In the 1904 Summer Olympics conducted in St. Louis, basketball was featured as an exhibition sport. The same year in Edgerton, according to Beckering, men and women began playing basketball on an intramural basis, either in Woodman Hall or upstairs in the Meacham Store. The competitive sites were determined by the anticipated turnout, with anyone above the age of ten charged fifteen cents to help defray the expenses and pay for the girls' uniforms.

Basketball's popularity spread rapidly throughout the nation, with high school systems being a major area of growth. A progressive Edgerton established a school system in 1879 on the A.A. Dodge farm and three years later constructed a school in Edgerton proper, but it was limited to elementary and middle-school ages. High schools were major conduits for basketball in the formative years, but Edgerton didn't have a high school until 1911, and in 1912 the town voted in favor of a new brick school.

The brick Edgerton Public grade and high school building was opened in 1913.

Details about Edgerton's early basketball history are sketchy. The first team was established somewhere between 1910 and 1912 and included Ray Delaney, Lawrence Meacham, Virgil Ashbough, Kenneth Kingsley, Fletcher Meacham, Donald Saum, Cleon Snow, and Alfred Ashbough. This is believed to have been the first of many Edgerton independent contingents composed of young adults and teens from town and country in the early years, and later former high school players and faculty competed against neighboring towns, Negro and Sons of David barnstorming teams, and state all-star groups such as the Golden Gopher alumni. Perhaps because people of color were unique to the area, the games attracted overflowing crowds including a 1938 contest which Edgerton won 43 to 37 over a team advertised as being the Globe Trotters, but more than likely a satellite team to the marquee Harlem Globe Trotters who played a big-time schedule in large-city venues and against high-profile professional teams.

In February of 1912, residents voted on a $16,000 bond for a new eight-room school building. Construction began the same year and by 1913 Edgerton students occupied a new two-floor, eight-room school in which grades one through eight attended classes on the first level, the remaining four grades on the second. The school gymnasi-

Edgerton's first basketball team was formed in 1910 included: Back row: Ray Delaney, Lawrence Meacham, Virgil Ashbough, Kenneth Kingsley; front row: Fletcher Meacham, Donald Saum, Cleon Snow, and Alfred Ashbough.

um was in the basement and would remain the home to Edgerton basketball until 1936-1937 when a $12,613.43 auditorium-gymnasium was erected on the school's south side.

In the winter of 1913, approximately six months before Edgerton's new school was opened, Northfield's Carleton College would be host to the first Minnesota state basketball tournament. Carleton College officials organized the competitive format and requested high schools to submit their season records, and from the list of applicants they selected thirteen teams including Austin, Blue Earth, Faribault, Fosston, Grand Rapids, Madison, Mankato, Mountain Lake, Plainview, Red Wing, Stillwater, Willmar, and Luverne, the latter only eighteen miles southwest of Edgerton. In Carleton's new Sayles-Hill Gymnasium, Fosston defeated Mountain Lake 29 to 27 for what was described as the "mythical" state championship. The inaugural competition attracted little media and fan attention, but high school administrators were impressed and joined

The Edgerton Public gymnasium was added in time for the 1936-1937 school year.

forces with Carleton in establishing eligibility rules, modifying the selection process, and organizing the tournament which continued to be played in Sayles-Hill Gymnasium. The field was cut to nine teams in 1914 when qualifying began in nine congressional districts, the fifth district composed of Minneapolis schools being excluded.

Carleton was host to the tournament through 1922, but in 1916 the Minnesota State High School League was organized and began to sanction the event. The tournament fields ranged from ten to sixteen teams until 1925 when the MSHSL established a qualifying system that included thirty-two districts and eight regions. St. Paul Mechanic Arts defeated Buffalo 20 to 8 in what might be considered the first official title game.

World War I soldiers Leonard Scott, Milo Brooks, Kenneth Kingsley, and Clay Baldwin. Kingsley entered service in April 1917, was deployed overseas April 1918, and died July 1918 in St. Nazaire, France.

EDGERTON

At this point, Edgerton High School was just playing catch-up from World War I. While all Americans were focused on the Great War, Edgerton was a small town that had neither the population nor resources to support both the nation's battles and school expansion. They were devoted to the Red Cross and other war-related organizations and activities. Some of the community's young men were involved in combat, one being Kenneth Kingsley, a member of the town's charter basketball team and who was killed in France in July 1918. Nationally, American Legion posts were established the same year to honor the soldiers who served in the war, and in August 1918 Edgerton founded Kingsley Post Number 42. Cliff Peterson, who lost his left arm in the war, was selected post commander in a unanimous vote.

Once peace was restored, Edgerton's attention returned to the community and its educational system, and in 1920 Ernest O. Nickerson began a twenty-eight-year tenure

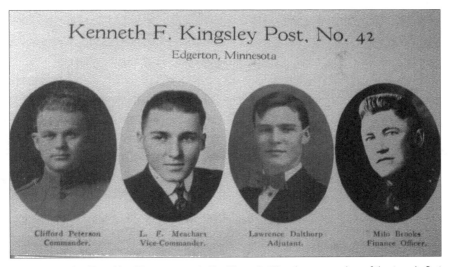

Edgerton Legion Post No. 42 was named after Kenneth Kingsley, a member of the town's first basketball team who was killed in France in 1918. Clifford Peterson, who lost an arm in combat in the Argonne-Meuse Drive in France, became the Edgerton Legion post's first commander.

as the school superintendent. Nickerson proved to be a visionary, developing a strong academic curriculum but leaving ample room for extracurricular activities. In addition to his administration and teaching duties, he coached boys and girls basketball and helped develop programs involving music, art, and drama. Edgerton High attained state accreditation in 1922 and the next year he enrolled the school into the Minnesota State High School League. Nickerson coached the first Edgerton varsity team a year before the program became an MSHSL activity, and according to an *Enterprise* report the basketball team went 2 and 0, defeating Jasper 9 to 3 and Wilmont by an undisclosed score.

Nickerson hired William Dehner to coach the boys the next season and while he guided the girls team which played the six-player, half-court basketball that was popular throughout much of Minnesota in the late 1920s through the 1930s. Girls basketball was popular and no more so than in Grand Meadow, a small southern town where the girls commanded statewide attention from 1929 through 1939 when they compiled a 94 and 0 record against teams from Minnesota and Iowa. During that span of years Edgerton girls had a winning record nine of eleven years and the program was healthy. In 1934 with a record of ten wins and two losses, coach Marie Eng and a team comprised of Alma Brower, Bea Gertz, Margaret Jolink, Marie Scholten, Angie Schnyder, Evelyn Stevens, Florence Tolsma, and Hermina Westera, captured the first district championship. In 1937 and 1938 it was difficult to determine district champions because of the girls basketball status. The 1937 team won a district tournament at Luverne, and only Dorothy Bacon, Pearl Stevens, and Jeanette Westera graduated before the 1938 team had a similar season, one year before the state board of education instructed high schools to abandon schoolgirl competition. The explanation was that recreational sports were more wholesome and inviting for more girls than were competitive activities. Some skeptics, however, insist that the skimpier uniforms that became fashionable in the thirties were too revealing.

Meanwhile, basketball for boys continued to thrive in popularity and schedules were expanding. Nickerson was followed by three different coaches in three years—Dehner going 3 and 7, Rick Raque 6 and 8—but Harry Gulbrandson arrived in 1924 and stuck around for four seasons as the principal and basketball coach. His first team was 8 and 6, followed by a lackluster 4 and 8, but he finished with 9 and 4 and 12 and 4 seasons before resigning in 1928, and his replacement, James H. Brovold, inherited a program with some stability and momentum.

1938 Edgerton Girls Team (left to right): Lewella De Koekkoek, Delvie Van Ort, Rose Marie Jacobs, Kathryn Verdoom, Geraldine DeJong, Kathryn Kooiman, Irma Snyder, Ruth Brooks, Lois Broekhuis, Mary Templeman, Helen Broekhuis, and Coach Ruby Rupner.

The new principal and coach, who answered to J.H. or "Brov" rather than James, increased the stability and maintained the momentum for most of the next twenty years, an era in which the fatherly figure, popular among both students and parents, earned the designation of "Mr. Basketball" in Edgerton and surrounding areas.

Brovold, twenty-one, was a recent graduate of St. Olaf College, just across town from Carleton in Northfield. The Edgerton newcomer who taught most every subject in addition to being principal and coach, was a former college football and baseball letterman, but didn't play basketball. When asked by a reporter from the *St. Paul Pioneer Press* why he hadn't played basketball, the 5-foot-8 personable Brovold smiled and said that he had been "too short to cut the mustard" on the court. The coach did, however, demonstrate a keen acumen and finished his first season 10 and 5 with a team that included Henry Vanderbush, Harris Meacham, Bernard Van Roekel, James Roelofs, Orson

J.H. Brovold, a St. Olaf College graduate, coached his first Edgerton team in 1928-1929.

EDGERTON

Millis, Walter Ellgen, Bill De Mots, and Joe Huisken. The solid finish would be the first of twelve winning seasons in the sixteen he coached, a 20 and 2 mark in 1939-1940, the hallmark campaign of a career in which he won 178 games and lost ninety-three. The twenty-victory season remained the program's standard of excellence until the Flying Dutchmen's state championship season in 1960.

Brovold's career was interrupted by World War II when he was a U.S. Army captain from the spring of 1942 through the fall of 1945. His wartime hiatus represented the only days he missed as an administrator, teacher, and coach during his time at Edgerton High. The man described by former player Clarence Graphenteen as "a good coach and a good man" coached two more seasons after he returned from the war, stepping aside to concentrate on school administration and teaching after the 1947 District 8 Tournament. He continued both roles until 1958, then resigned as the principal and became the school guidance counselor. He retired from full-time education in 1971, an occasion that prompted congratulatory letters from state and national notables including President Richard M. Nixon, Minnesota Governor Wendell Anderson, and then Minnesota Senator Hubert Humphrey. Brovold became a willing substitute teacher and remained a community fixture until his death in 1981.

Together, Brovold and Nickerson provided yeoman duty in the improvement and expansion of Edgerton High's athletic program. They generated support for the construction of a new auditorium, which replaced the school's smaller basement gymnasium in the fall of 1936-1937, and two years later played an integral role in adopting the school's "Flying Dutchmen" nickname. Under their watch, and with the assistance of Eldon (Docky) Ford, a savvy basketball player and superb quarterback, Edgerton launched a six-man football team in 1939 and joined the Tri-County League in February of 1940.

Edgerton had two losing basketball records in the three seasons Brovold was gone, but he quickly got the program back on track. His final two teams went 12 and 5 and 19 and 5 and the four coaches who followed him endured only three losing seasons despite the emergence of Southwest Christian High in the early 1950s. Nickerson was in California when Edgerton won the 1960 state championship, having moved to San Diego upon his retirement in 1948, but Brovold—whose only regret was having never produced a District 8 title—still was around to enjoy the triumph.

"After waiting thirty-two years, it finally happened," he said emotionally after watching Edgerton defeat Worthington for the title.

The lengthy wait was not a reflection on the long-time coach, his predecessors, or the community. Tiny Edgerton was never the epicenter of southwestern basketball, just a town with a profound passion and competitive spirit for the game but too often outnumbered by the opposition. Six towns were larger than Edgerton in District 8 and none had to share its available athletic talent with another high school. In fact, around the mid 1950s Edgerton's Southwest Christian surpassed Edgerton's public school in enrollment and attracted enough good local talent to be competitive in regional parochial play. The two schools scrimmaged against one another until the mid-1970s, when Southwest Christian foined the Tri-County Conference. According to the *Enterprise*, Southwest won the first meeting.

By the time Edgerton joined the MSHSL, Luverne's basketball program had more than a decade head start on most District 8 towns. The Cardinals won seventeen basketball district titles from 1927 through 1958 and when they didn't win, Worthington or Pipestone generally prevailed. Several times smaller towns eliminated Edgerton in District 8 play, but Luverne, Pipestone, Worthington, and Slayton were most often the Flying Dutchmen's source of frustration.

Until Edgerton's epic 1960 flourish, the state's perennial Cinderella was Mountain Lake, whose population remained around 1,800 through most of the 1940s and 1950s. The Lakers were a state force early, finishing second three times in the first five state tournaments held in Carleton and they won the 1939 state title. From that point, Mountain Lake became a frequent state tournament sweetheart, but the larger schools in Region I and VII and the Minneapolis powers in Region V took charge. Mankato and Mountain Lake dominated Region II through the years, with Mankato qualifying for the state fifteen times through 1959 and Mountain Lake thirteen times through 1952.

In the post-World War II era, Region III's Lynd—population 250 and less than an hour up the road from Edgerton—became the all-time Minnesota state tourney overachiever when it finished second to mighty Austin in 1946. In 1957, Pemberton, a Region II town with a population of less than 100, became the smallest town ever to qualify for a post season trip to Williams Arena. Even in District 8, Edgerton's longtime rival Jasper, population 850, upstaged Edgerton in terms of small-town achievement by winning two district titles, the second at the expense of the Flying Dutchmen in the 1959 district final.

For believers in omens, Brovold's first season at Edgerton could have been interpreted as a sign that nothing would come easy for its high school basketball program. After finishing the regular season with a winning record, Edgerton entered the district, which in 1929 featured a sig-

EDGERTON

nificantly more complicated and arduous format than in later years. The sub-district was conducted in one day with each team playing at least two games, then the two surviving teams advanced to the intra-district final played in one day the following weekend.

Edgerton's quest began on a bitterly cold morning in which a snowstorm had made most area roads impassable. Rather than rescheduling the games, school officials used Mike Jasper's bobsled to transport the eight-man team to Hardwick, a two-and-one-half-hour journey in which players rotated positions—six in the sled and two walking behind. The team was fortunate that state rules allowed for only eight men on a roster.

Once in Hardwick, the team was transferred into a Model T Ford with side curtains and the team and coach were transported to Luverne where they arrived twenty-five minutes before the morning game's tip-off. Edgerton defeated Beaver Creek 38 to 24 then headed to the Manitou Hotel to rest before their night game. The hotel stay was infinitely more comfortable than the trek from Edgerton to Luverne, but a far cry from being in the lap of luxury. The eight players were assigned to one room, so small that to afford them all sleeping space, Walt "Spike" Ellgen was relegated to the bathtub, perhaps the most comfortable spot in the house. Hills defeated Edgerton 27 to 15 in the night game witnessed by a small delegation of loyal Edgerton fans who braved the elements, reaching Luverne by way of Woodstock and Pipestone. The players returned home that night, chilled and tired, but knowing their morning victory had assured them a berth in the following weekend's one-day intra-divisional tournament.

Road conditions improved only slightly during the week, but the team's Saturday trip to Slayton was a breeze in contrast to the previous Saturday. The players rode to Woodstock in the back of a cream truck and then boarded a train for Slayton. Edgerton beat Walnut Grove 18 to 9 in the opener, defeated Brewster 25 to 21 in the second game, but once again lost to Hills 38 to 31 in the championship. Edgerton received the sportsmanship trophy, deservedly so, since there was no threat of a mutiny during either road trip, but the honor was decided by a coin toss. Hills advanced to district play the next weekend in Worthington where Brovold's hometown school was eliminated by Pipestone 8 to 6.

Snowstorms weren't the only obstacle that had an impact on Edgerton basketball, then and in later years. When the waters from the Chanarmbe and Rock rivers overflowed at a time in which basketball interest crested, bridges sometimes were washed away and made travel in and out of town difficult, if not dangerous.

In 1929-1930, Edgerton finished 10 and 5 for a second straight year and played in another sub-district marathon, requiring four games in three days. The Dutchmen defeated Hills 19 to 17 on Friday, then returned Saturday for a three-game set in which the locals defeated Okabena 22 to 17 in the opener, lost to Adrian 24 to 13 and defeated Magnolia 32 to 20 in the consolation game. Datus Beckering, a second-team all-district selection, provided little or no help against Adrian because he was ill after being hit in the stomach with a ball in the Okabena game. Adrian breezed through the tournament 3 and 0 and advance to the district finals.

On the heels of the two 10 and 5 seasons came a two-year swoon of 4 and 10 and 6 and 10, but the locals turned things around in 1932-1933 when they finished 15 and 2. The record included wins over larger foes Luverne, Pipestone, and Slayton, but in the district tiny Magnolia spoiled what had the makings of a dream season. The next

The 1934 Edgerton boys team included (alphabetically) Russell Dethmers, Don Krosschell, Ernest Schulhouse, Smith (not available), Blaine Trichel, Allen Youngsma. Back (left) E.O. Nickerson, and (right) Coach J.H. Brovold.

season after losing only two seniors (Ray Vanderbush and Jim Baker) Edgerton finished 16 and 3, and a district title was a possibility until Allen Youngsma sprained his ankle.

Edgerton kept on winning the next two years with John Bouma, Wayne Jacobs, Don Krosschell, Lester Rolfs, and Fred Vanderstoep. From 1933-1936 Edgerton won seventy-five percent of all their games and had a record of fifty wins and only sixteen losses.

Through the remainder of the thirties, Edgerton's enrollment grew—the Class of '35 having a school-record twenty-five graduates—and the basketball program became more competitive, but Luverne firmly ruled the district and region, qualifying for the Minnesota state tournament in 1935, 1936, and 1938. The 1939-1940 Edgerton team with Arnold Klindt, Darrell Strassburg, and anchored by Stanley

Roetman, Marv Krosschell, and Eldon (Docky) Ford won an unprecedented twenty victories with two defeats. Unfortunately one of the losses was a 29 to 27 District 8 loss to Luverne whom the Flying Dutchmen defeated 25 to 24 during the regular season. Roetman had a miserable night at the free throw line in the loss, hitting only three of nine attempts, and Edgerton's last-gasp field-goal attempt near the buzzer missed the mark. During a span from 1938-1940 Edgerton's win-loss record was 50 and 12 winning eighty percent of all games.

Brovold coached two more seasons, the first a so-so 9 and 6 and the second an equally tepid 7 and 10, but interest in basketball was overshadowed by the prospect of war. Early in the second season, the Japanese bombed Pearl Harbor and President Franklin Delano Roosevelt declared war on Japan and Germany, and when the 1943 season began, Brovold was a captain in the U.S. Air Force and Raymond Oliver began

The members of the 1937-1938 basketball team were (left to right): Eldon Ford, Donald Jones, Stan Roetman, Arnold Klindt, Alvin Muilenburg, Arnold Bolluyt, Roland DeJong, and Marv Krosschell. Two years later, Ford, Roetman, and Krosschell were part of a Flying Dutchman team that finished with an unprecedented 20 and 2 record.

what would be a two-year stay in Edgerton. Oliver's first team went 10 and 2 and ended with a 28 to 23 sub-district loss to Jasper, a game in which Edgerton led until star Billy Brooks was sidelined by an injury. Edgerton dipped to 5 and 7 the next season, a season that abruptly ended in a 23 to 21 sub-district loss to Beaver Creek, and Fulda became the smallest town in District 8 to win a basketball title. Even the usually supportive *Edgerton Enterprise* made no attempt to conceal its frustration, grousing editorially, "After the years of good basketball teams and good games, our high school team hit the very bottom."

The reaction, however, had to be linked in part to war fatigue. America had been mired in World War II since December 1941, and although U.S. forces were gaining on both fronts, casualties were enormous and neither Germany nor Japan demonstrated a scintilla of willingness to surrender. When coach N.B. Hoyme and the Flying Dutchmen finished 6 and 9 the following winter, area fans and the *Enterprise* were distracted by the prospect of peace and mourning the loss of nearly a half million American lives.

Brovold returned in 1945 and resumed his administrative, teaching and coaching duties, but nine area young men were among the casualties: John Christians, coast artillery, January 1943; Pilot Ray Vanderbush 1943; Pfc. Peter Lorenzen, July 1944; Pfc. John Zylstra, September 1944; S. Sgt. John Van Bockel, September 1944; S. Sgt. Elmer Jelgerhuis, December 1944; Pvt. Leslie Brink, February 1945; Second Lt. John Romkema, March 1945; and Quartermaster First Class Marion Schaap, July 1945. Ray Vanderbush played basketball in 1933. Jelgerhuis and Romkema were former Edgerton players who were basketball starters in 1940-1941. Romkema was considered one of Edgerton's finest basketball players of the pre-war era.

High school basketball continued through World War II, with newspaper game articles and box scores documenting the Edgerton High's lean years during the turbulent period and the almost instant revival once peace was declared. In retrospect, the long-term Flying Dutchmen's future could be traced in part by non-sports related news items and a look at Pipestone County's birth records.

Southwest Christian School was opened in 1916, but didn't offer a high school curriculum until 1939 and that was only for freshman and sophomores. Not long after the war, SWC officials announced plans for a four-year high school which opened in 1950. Three years later, twelve students participated in the school's first commencement and the senior high enrollment continued to increase. How did parents decide where to send their children, Edgerton Public or the Southwest Christian School? One longtime citizen put it best, explaining: "I guess it just depended on who married who." Certainly, athletics was not the major priority because the basketball pool was being split down the middle, paring Edgerton Public's competitive potential.

Conversely, the 1960 championship team was in its infancy in the early forties, literally. Birth dates of Edgerton's state tournament team ranged from October 1941 through December 1944, the newcomers including Bob Wiarda, Dean Verdoes, Daryl Stevens, Dean Veenhof, Darrell Kreun, LeRoy Graphenteen, Jim Roos, Tom Warren, Norm Muilenburg, Bob Dykstra, D.J. Fey, and Larry Schoolmeester.

Verdoes, Kreun, and Graphenteen each had at least one brother who preceded him in the Flying Dutchmen fold, but while some of the names remained the same, the late forties and fifties would be a time for major change, marked by highs and lows before the dawning of the Edgerton Legend.

CHAPTER TWO
Post Nickerson and Brovold and World War II

When Edgerton's 1947-1948 school term began, Edgerton athletics had undergone a major transition. Superintendent E.O. Nickerson and Principal J.H. Brovold were still the school's primary administrators, but Nickerson was preparing to retire after the ensuing school year, and Brovold, who had orchestrated Flying Dutchman football and basketball for most of the previous twenty years, relinquished his coaching duties. In the next nine years, the Flying Dutchmen basketball program had four different coaches, each upholding the

Edgerton Superintendent E.O. Nickerson.

school's winning tradition but also unable to purge the post season curse that haunted Brovold throughout his lengthy tenure.

Robert Westergard came first, hired by Nickerson off the South Dakota State College campus. The two-sport Jackrabbit standout and former World War II Marine Corps pilot proved to be a bargain at $2,600 a year, teaching two subjects and coaching two sports. He produced Tri-County championships in football and basketball, but resigned in the spring to rejoin the Marine Corps, serving three years before launching a thirty-year career in the airlines industry. He never coached another season after leaving Edgerton.

Westergard's 1947 football team was 6 and 0, Edgerton's first undefeated season since the Flying Dutchmen went 8 and 0 in the school's inaugural season. Edgerton won the Tri-County title in six-man football and finished the season defeating Jasper in an eleven-man

The 1947 Edgerton football team. Left to right: Assistant Coach J.H. Brovold, Casey DeJong, Tom Lucas, Everett Lensink, Ivan Dale Hankins, Leroy Tinklenberg, unknown player, Louis Vander Plaats, Clarence Graphenteen, and Coach Bob Westegard.

game. The basketball team went 19 and 5, the second most wins in school history, and after claiming the Tri-County title defeated Pipestone and Worthington in the District 8 tournament before losing 33 to 29 to Slayton in the championship game. The Flying Dutchmen defeated Slayton during the regular season. Westergard's records were particularly impressive considering that he was an accidental coach more interested in flying airplanes than mentoring the Flying Dutchmen. Call it a case of bad timing in the eyes of the former Marine Corps captain who resigned at the end of World War II and returned to SDSC to complete his education.

"When I got out of the Marine Corps [November 1945] the airlines were hiring a lot of people," said Westergard, a South Dakota native. "But I was more interested in getting back to hunt pheasants. It was probably one of the most foolish things I've ever done. By the time I graduated all the [airline] jobs were gone. I guess it was in the spring of my season [in Edgerton] that a Marine Corps colonel I knew found me an assignment, and so I went back into the Marine Corps. I forget what I got paid, but it was a helluva lot more than I made in Edgerton."

Westergard never returned to Edgerton, but sixty years later he fondly recalled his nine months in the southwestern Minnesota town. He said he was blessed with exceptional athletic talent for such a small community and recalled the names of many players he coached. He referred to fullback Tom Lucas and quarterback Casey DeJong as two major players in the football season and discussed the basketball starters and key reserves as if he had posted a roster earlier in the day, a roster that included Everett Lensink, Leroy Tinklenberg, Ivan Dale Hankins, Clarence Graphenteen, Louis Vander Plaats, DeJong, and Lucas.

EDGERTON

The players liked the charismatic coach with several visiting him the next season in the Twin Cities.

"We had some good kids, I tell you; a few were college material," Westergard said. "If I had gotten there a year earlier and if we had had [Louis] Vander Plaats the whole season, we would have had a very good team, but we lost him early because of a knee injury. Lensink was our best player. He had a nice left-handed shot. I really felt bad for him in the final game [against Slayton] because his shots would just roll around the rim but wouldn't go in."

Edgerton did a remarkable job against the big towns, beating Pipestone twice and Slayton once during the regular season, losing to the South Dakota State "B" team by a point, and surprising Worthington 41 to 35 in District 8 play. In the post season loss to Slayton, the Flying Dutchmen overcome an early ten-point deficit, but then squandered the spirited rally by missing several easy shots in the final minute.

"That was our third game in as many nights and our legs were pretty rubbery by the end of the game," DeJong said. "We simply ran out of gas. In those days we didn't know how to use the clock to our advantage."

Casey DeJong and Everett Lensink made the "all-district" team, and it was Lensink's second consecutive year.

While Westergard was flying in the South Pacific, his eventual replacement Dick Hayden was raising a family and working part time for the Minneapolis bus line while attending the University of Minnesota. Hayden, a Minnesota native whose high school days were split between Minnesota and Iowa, attempted to enlist in the military during World War II, but was rejected because of his asthma. For a while he played semi-professional baseball and

Edgerton principal and coach J.H. Brovold

pondered a professional career until he injured his throwing arm. He continued playing baseball while teaching and coaching at Edgerton and was a first baseman and pitcher on Woodstock's 1950 State B tournament team.

At 6-foot-4 with the frame of an NFL lineman, Hayden had an imposing presence. He lacked the charisma of his predecessor, but he quickly commanded the respect of his students and players. Unlike Westergard, who was an "accidental coach," Hayden was a committed teacher-coach who remained in education for thirty-two years: five in Edgerton, three in Dassel, and the remaining twenty-four in Howard Lake, where he achieved the majority of his success.

Hayden is remembered as a knowledgeable coach who worked well with his players, a man who stressed fundamentals and provided them well-prepared game plans compiled from many nighttime scouting trips. By most accounts, he was an affable individual off the court but prone to be an official's greatest nightmare in competition. He generally brandished a white shower room towel during games, waving it, twisting it, and occasionally throwing it on the floor. Casey DeJong recalls one occasion when Hayden hurled the towel against a gymnasium wall about ten feet from the floor, then marching down the sideline to retrieve it.

1948-1949 mainstays were John Beukelman, Sid Koster, Fred Baldwin, and Casey DeJong.

"He was a good coach and a nice guy, but he could be an ornery sonofagun," Arnie Graphenteen said of the man for whom he played three varsity seasons. "He wanted a certain amount of you and he usually got it. Brovold was the assistant, but he didn't say much . . . I think maybe he was afraid of [Hayden].

"He also got after officials a lot. I don't remember him ever getting kicked out of a game, but he'd let them know what he thought. Sometimes, all he had to do was give them a dirty look."

Hayden coached three sports at Edgerton, producing respectable records in football and basketball. His five-year

Minnesota's tallest front line in 1948-1949. Left to right: 6-foot-7 Gerrit "High Pockets" Wensink, 6-foot-8 Peter Gruys, and 6-foot-5 Dennis McVenes.

record in football was 21 and 11, highlighted by a 5 and 2 Tri-County season in 1948. In basketball, Hayden opened 16 and 6 and 17 and 3 and finished 71 and 36, one of the program's most successful periods, but his tenure was as frustrating as it was successful.

Edgerton opened modestly in 1948-1949, winning four games and losing three, but the Flying Dutchmen, anchored by 6-foot-5 Dennis McVenes, Casey DeJong, Fred Baldwin, and Dean Gruys suddenly caught fire. They surprised the Pipestone Arrows 45 to 28 in their eighth game and rolled into District 8 play with a 13 and 5 record and abundant momentum reflected in their first two post season victories, a 46 to 21 romp over Beaver Creek and a 67 to 14 trouncing of Magnolia. After defeating Pipestone for the second time, a 40 to 34 semifinal triumph, the lone obstacle looming between Edgerton and its first district title was Worthington.

The Trojans, representing the district's largest school, slowed the game's tempo and the two teams were locked in a deliberate tug of war throughout, despite the foul problems that beset McVenes and Baldwin. Edgerton wrangled a four-point lead late in the final period and

Hayden sent McVenes back on to the court to help secure the victory, but the lanky center quickly fouled out and Worthington's last-minute spurt earned the Trojans a 36 to 32 victory. In the Region 2 Tournament, Worthington defeated East Chain in overtime and played Mankato even for three quarters before losing 29 to 27.

Despite losing in his final high school game, Casey DeJong considered the previous season's district setback to have been far more demoralizing. "We really thought that we should have won the Slayton game," DeJong said reaching back to 1948. "In the 1949 district we got a good draw, but I believe we were the underdog going into the Worthington game, and from what I remember we were playing uphill most of the game."

The 1949-1950 Flying Dutchmen were one of the school's most celebrated teams, with a 17 and 3 record and the statewide attention focused on the trio of 6-foot-5 Dennis McVenes, 6-foot-7 Gerrit "High Pockets" Wensink, and 6-foot-8 Peter Gruys, cousin of returning starter Dean Gruys. The *Minneapolis Star and Tribune* did a feature on the trio,

The 1949-1950 team. Left to right: front: Chuck Hoffman, Arnie Graphenteen, Albertus Schelhaas, Duane Westenberg, Jerold Schoolmeester; back: Coach Hayden, Owen Pool, Dean Gruys, Dennis McVenes, Peter Gruys, Gerrit Wensink, Milford Stevens, and Roland Beckering.

Hayden has half-time talk with his 1949-1950 team.

proclaiming that Edgerton had the state's tallest team, not an outlandish assumption considering that the average center stood around 6-foot-1 or 6-foot-2. Hayden seldom put all three on the court simultaneously because Wensink and Gruys were relative newcomers to the game, so he alternated them as starters. McVenes, Arnie Graphenteen, Chuck Hoffman, and Dean Gruys were consistently in the starting lineup. Wensink and Peter Gruys contributed little to Edgerton's 980 to 580 scoring advantage, but Wensink showed some offensive potential toward the end and both provided welcome rebounding support.

In addition to the cast of returnees, team depth was enhanced by several members from the previous season's 15 and 2 "B" team, and the community partisans waxed optimistic. The Flying Dutchmen justified that abounding enthusiasm by winning their first eleven games, two in the Tri-County Tournament and a 49 to 34 romp over neighborhood rival Pipestone. In nineteen regular-season starts, Edgerton lost only two games, and both were to out-of-state teams, a six-point setback against Iowa's Hull High and a seven-point loss to South Dakota's Flandreau Indians. Hull matched up nicely with Edgerton in size, averaging 6-foot-4 across the front, and the Flying Dutchmen wilted against the Flandreau Indians and their relentless up-tempo style.

Several days after completing an undefeated Tri-County championship run, the Flying Dutchmen confidently entered their district tournament opener against Pipestone, a pairing determined in a January draw. Edgerton defeated Pipestone in the regular season, coming from behind with a fourth-quarter surge, and the Flying Dutchmen owned a three-game winning streak over the Arrows going back to 1948. Edgerton fell behind fourteen points early and rallied to catch the Arrows but sixteen missed free throws in twenty-nine attempts spelled the difference in a 37 to 29 loss. Adding insult to injury, Pipestone was forced into overtime before defeating Hills in the next round, a team that Edgerton defeated by thirty-one points less than two weeks earlier.

"We beat them during the regular season and I think we had a little bit of a big head . . . thought that we had the game won before we played it," Arnie Graphenteen said. "We also picked a bad time to have a cold shooting night . . . I know that I didn't shoot that well. Dean Gruys kept us in the game for a while, but they pretty much took it to us."

A post season *Edgerton Enterprise* comment perhaps reflected the community's frustration: "Edgerton fans are not too disturbed over the upset—they've become accustomed to it," the article read, alluding to the second upset loss in three seasons.

Edgerton had some gratifying moments beyond Hayden's first two seasons. He would produce three more winning records and win seven post season games, but the Flying Dutchmen regular-season success waned and the inexplicable post season setbacks continued to plague them.

EDGERTON

In Hayden's third season, Edgerton finished 13 and 10 and won the Tri-County title, but beyond victories over Pipestone and Lester High from Iowa—a game in which Dean Gruys scored a school-record twenty-seven—the Flying Dutchmen struggled in the conference. They defeated Beaver Creek and Pipestone in their first district tournament games, but bowed out in a 30 to 29 loss to Jasper in the west Sub-District finals when Jasper scored the winning basket with two seconds remaining.

Edgerton won its first four games in Hayden's fourth season including a 33 to 31 victory over Slayton coached by Duane Baglien, who several years later would take Fergus Falls to the state tournament and in the mid-sixties guided Edina to an unprecedented three consecutive Minnesota championships in the one-divisional era. Les Graphenteen and Darwin Wassink were the team leaders, but future Edgerton great John Fransen assumed a greater offensive role as the season progressed.

Edgerton won nine of its first eleven games in Hayden's final season. The Flying Dutchmen won the Tri-County title, but the Dutchmen lost five games of their last eight contests, a lapse underscored by a 61 to 39 season-ending drubbing at Luverne. The Flying Dutchmen opened district play with comfortable victories over Jasper and Magnolia, only to endure another post season loss to Pipestone after defeating the Arrows in the regular season. On the horizon was a much greater concern involving Flying Dutchmen basketball. The Christian School's enrollment rapidly was increasing, the growth having a significant impact on Edgerton High and its basketball program. In fact, Christian School basketball became extremely competitive in the latter half of the decade.

When Hayden left for Dassel, he wasn't running away from a challenge. His move was based almost exclusively on finances and an opportunity to move closer to friends and relatives in the Twin Cities. Beyond his three-year stay in Dassel, he fashioned an outstanding record in Howard Lake, winning eighty-five percent of his games over twelve years despite scheduling several non-conference games against Minneapolis schools each year and competing in District 20, dominated by perennial state power Willmar. Howard Lake had two twenty-win seasons, with the 1959 Lakers losing to Willmar in the district final and his 1962 team advancing to the Region V tournament. In 1958, the year after Roosevelt won its second straight state title, Howard Lake defeated the Teddies.

"He wasn't a competitor, he was a winner. I can't remember us having a losing basketball season," former Howard Lake school board member Don Gutzke said. "And he was not only a good coach, he was a gentleman who was

The 1951-1952 team. Left to right: back row: John Brands, John Fransen, Andrew Klumper, John Brouwer, Robert Tinklenberg, Darwin Wassink; front row: Coach Hayden, Duane Kreun, Eddie Hulstein, David Elson, Arnie Graphenteen, and manager Henry Klumper.

well-respected by everyone for his leadership in our community and throughout the area.

"As a member of the Howard Lake school board, I attended dozens of meetings with Dick Hayden and it was a joy to see how his peers responded to him."

Bill Standly had metropolitan roots, having graduated from Minneapolis Roosevelt High and—after a military tour in World War II—the University of Minnesota so one might assume that he and his wife, Fran, experienced a sense of isolation when they arrived in Edgerton. That could not have been further from the truth. From the U of M, Standly went to North Dakota where he taught and coached two seasons at Dodge, population 125. Southwest Christian hadn't begun an all-inclusive high school curricu-

The 1953-1954 team. Left to right: Back row: John Bylsma, John Brands, John Fransen, Duane Kreun, Duane Pool, Bruce Schoolmeester; Front row: Lloyd Wassink, Nick Veenhof, Jerry Van Peursem, Carroll Kreun, and Melvin Lorenzen.

lum until 1950, but by the time Standly arrived the parochial school's nine through twelve enrollment was equal to that of Edgerton Public and the two were in an evenly matched tug of war for local athletes.

Standly had the good fortune in his first season that he had John Fransen, a 6-foot-1 forward who despite not having played organized ball until eighth grade developed into one of southwest Minnesota's most prolific scorers. He scored 1,017 points during his high-school career. Led by Fransen, Edgerton won six of its first seven games, a mercurial start highlighted by victories over the run-and-gun Flandreau Indians, then cooled slightly to finish the regular season 14 and 5. Edgerton lost its final game, but it was a three-point loss to mighty Luverne and excitement abounded. After Edgerton, where he scored a career 1,017 points, Fransen attended and played basketball at Pepperdine College, a California power in that era. Anything was possible with Fransen, averaging approximately twenty-five points per game that included a record thirty-three against Flandreau. Pipestone, however, quickly ended Edgerton's tournament dreams, defeating the Flying Dutchmen by seventeen points.

"There wasn't that much scouting in those days, but they did know that I was scoring more than half our team points," Fransen said. "They threw a zone press at us and every time I got the ball I had someone on each side of me and if I wanted to shoot I had to go outside.

"I couldn't find a groove. Normally, on game days, I'd work at the bakery from four o'clock to eight o'clock, but someone convinced the owner to give me the day off for some extra rest. I think that sort of knocked me out of my routine."

Standly faced a major rebuilding project the next season, having lost Fransen and three other senior starters. The second-year coach began the task with returning starting guard John Bylsma and a cast of unseasoned varsity reserves and "B" squad graduates, but while the Flying Dutchmen managed a winning season, 11 and 10, it was a season fraught with indignities. They finished with the poorest won-lost percentage since 1943. They never won more than two consecutive games. They scored more than fifty points only five times and in the program's lowest scoring effort since the end of World War II, they were pummeled 51 to 20 by Dell Rapids. In the district tournament, Edgerton went one-and-out for the second straight year in a 41 to 37 loss to Pipestone, marking the fourth time in six years the Arrows had eliminated them from post season play.

A more experienced Edgerton team bounced back in 1955-1956, but it was no quantum leap. Lloyd Wassink and Les Graphenteen shared scoring honors with 12.7 averages in a 13 and 10 season. The Flying Dutchmen ended the regular season in a twenty-seven point loss to Luverne and after defeating Beaver Creek and Jasper in district tournament games were eliminated by the Cardinals, 66 to 45, led by Jed Cooney's thirty-seven points.

When Standly resigned in the spring, he took with him a reputation as an excellent football man and a good person. Every year he took the football players to the cities to a Gopher game.

"He was a heckuva nice guy. I really liked him," Duane Kreun said. "He was a former University of Minnesota football player who knew how to teach blocking and tackling, but he didn't seem to know much about set plays in basketball, things like pick and rolls. We more or less played a free-lance offense. When I got to college, it was really an eye opener because on almost every possession we had a set pattern."

Standly compiled a 17 and 2 with 1 tie football record at Edgerton, the school's finest three-year record since the program was organized in 1939. His final team finished 5 and 0 with 1 tie, only the third undefeated season in Flying Dutchmen history. In defense of Standly's modest basketball record, he was the first to compete with Southwest Christian for the town's better players—Bob Den Cote, Mike Vander Pol, George Huisken, and Donley Broekhuis were among the locals to choose SWC. And what basketball knowledge Standly appeared to lack while in Edgerton, he apparently acquired in the next several years.

From Edgerton he moved to Albert Lea, where he was an assistant "B" team coach for two seasons and a varsity assistant for another. In 1960, he received and accepted an offer from San Diego High to coach varsity basketball and compiled one of southern California's most impressive records in the decade.

Standly inherited a young team his first season that included future Minnesota Twin Craig Nettles and the

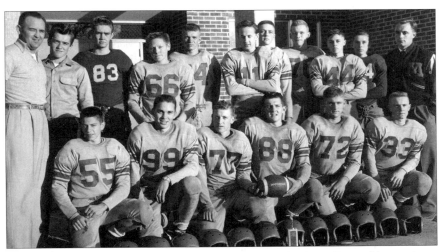

The 1955 football team. Back row: Coach Standly, Virg Tinklenberg, Duane Stevens, Larry Thorson, Eddie Veldhuizen, Archie Schnyders, Harris Tinklenberg, Norm Hendricks, Duane Landhuis, Clarence Tinklenberg, Assistant Ken Kielty; Front row: Carroll Westenberg, Lloyd Pool, Les Graphenteen, Lloyd Wassink, Dean Brockberg, and Bruce Schoolmeester.

Cavemen finished 10 and 14, the first of two losing seasons in his first three campaigns. But San Diego won nineteen games in 1963-1964 and the next season when his team went 24 and 9 and claimed the San Diego Section title, he was on his way. His hallmark season came in 1966-1967 when the Cavemen enjoyed an exhilarating 29 and 2 ride culminated by a San Diego Section title. They won their last fourteen games and broke Mount Miguel's sixteen-game winning streak to win the section title. San Diego High's season earned Standly both the Southern California and San Diego basketball coach of the year recognition. He retired in 1969 with a 172 and 86 record and combined with his tours in Dodge, North Dakota and Edgerton the soft-spoken coach won more than 230 high school basketball games.

Standly's marquee player from 1964 through 1967 was Oscar Foster, a 6-foot-7 sensation whom NBA Hall-of-Fame member Bill Walton once described as "one of San Diego's basketball legends." Foster, who compiled 1,766 points and a 3.3 grade point index in high school, received 185 college offers, accepting the one from the University of Minnesota. At a time when the NCAA prohibited freshman from varsity competition, Foster averaged 18.9 points per game for the Gopher freshman team, but he became homesick and transferred back to California. Foster attended the University of San Diego, but his career was devastated by psychological problems and he plummeted out of university life into the depths of San Diego's homeless population.

Ken Kielty spent most of his time as the "B" team coach and organizing a junior program, but did notice a lack of order in his predecessor's offense. He wasn't, however, surprised by Standly's basketball success in California.

"He didn't play basketball in high school or college," Kielty said of his fellow Roosevelt High alum, "and since he was coaching everything at Edgerton, he was limited in what he could do each season. But he obviously learned along the way. That's what you do if you are a good coach. He obviously enjoyed coaching basketball because he took an assistant's position at Albert Lea where he had a much better opportunity to learn."

And while Standly was learning in Albert Lea, Kielty was left to re-energize the Flying Dutchmen program, a task that the first-year coach found formidable and at times almost overwhelming, but in the end extremely gratifying.

CHAPTER THREE
The Building Years

Winning basketball never was what it was all about in Edgerton, a town where the major priorities were religion, family values, and work ethics. Conversely, it would be folly to imply that the community lacked an avid interest in the game and wasn't experiencing frustration.

Never mind that Edgerton public had never won a District 8 title, the Flying Dutchmen were losing their competitive edge. In the first seven seasons after World War II, they were 106 and 40 for a .723 won-lost percentage, but in a three-year span the Flying Dutchmen were 36 and 25 for a .591 percentage, and the future appeared bleak in light of the Christian School's rapid expansion.

One hundred and sixty miles away in Minneapolis, Ken Kielty, a University of Minnesota senior was completing his student coaching under C. Wayne Courtney at Roosevelt High, the city's largest public high school. Kielty was a starting Gopher outfielder the previous spring and had the option of seeking an extra year of eligibility, which he probably would have been granted in lieu of his nineteen-month state-side military tour during the Korean Conflict. Kielty began his education at Mankato State Teachers College and played two football seasons and one in baseball before his National Guard unit was called up in January 1951. Upon his discharge, he moved back to Minneapolis and enrolled in the University of Minnesota.

"I really enjoyed my time at Mankato, but I figured that with the GI bill and being able to live at home, college was much more affordable at the University of Minnesota," Kielty explained.

As appealing as it would have been to play another baseball season for Dick Siebert, a former major league first baseman and outstanding college coach from whom Kielty learned a great deal about coaching, Kielty didn't want to delay his graduation. He was almost twenty-five years old, married, the father of an infant son, Dan. His wife, Barbara, was pregnant with their second child. Professional baseball wasn't in his future, and he desperately needed a regular paycheck, so he graduated and signed a contract to teach and coach at Edgerton's public school.

A Twin Cities school would have seemed like a wise choice for Kielty, for he and his wife, a Washburn graduate, were born and raised in the shadows of the city skyline. He did inquire at the Minneapolis school district office, but no vacancies were posted and so he attended a campus job fair to see what was available in Minnesota or out-of-state. He had two interviews, one with a school district representative from Bakersfield, California, and a second with an Edgerton School District representative, and he ultimately received offers from both. Barb Kielty adamantly opposed a move halfway across the country away from family and friends, and the school year rapidly was approaching. Kielty knew a little about the small southwest Minnesota town from his former Mankato football teammate Casey DeJong, an Edgerton native, but he made the four-hour drive to get a firsthand look at the community, population 861 according to the 1950 census. He interviewed with superintendent Charles Gibson, who, after defining the job description— math teacher, head baseball coach, and football-basketball assistant—suggested that Kielty talk to basketball and football coach Bill Standly.

Standly spoke fondly of the community but candidly informed Kielty that the ensuing school year would be his last in Edgerton. He implied that if Kielty was interested in coaching basketball, the job would almost certainly be his for the asking. For the big-city young adult, the basketball opportunity was the caveat in his decision to sign a $3,700 contract with one of the smallest public schools in Pipestone County; in fact, soon to be the smaller high school in Edgerton where the Christian School enrollment was making a mercurial climb.

Kielty was first and foremost a baseball man who had played the game most of his life and was good enough to be a starting Big Ten outfielder and a prominent player in the tough Minneapolis Park Board League. In fact, he also coached high school baseball, and the Pipestone town-team baseball board recruited Kielty on a play-for-pay basis. Later, he was designated the team's player-manager, a position he held until leaving the area. Although he played basketball only briefly in high school and none in college, Kielty had a passion for the game and a strong grasp of fundamentals that he acquired from C. Wayne Courtney at Roosevelt where Kielty did his student coaching while attending the university. He also was a fan who acquired a profound fascination with the game from watching Gopher standouts Chuck Mencel and Dick Garmaker.

"I could have waited and probably gotten a job in Minneapolis, but it would have been at the junior high level," Kielty said. "Edgerton offered an opportunity to begin my coaching career much sooner than if I remained in the Minneapolis area. In addition to loving the sport, I liked the nature of coaching the sport. In baseball, you don't know when or even if you are going to practice because of the spring weather. In basketball you are inside and could set aside specific hours to practice, knowing that nothing was going to interfere."

The Kieltys were delighted by the welcome they received. Several families including their landlords, Thelma and Elmer Kooiman, were on hand to help them settle in, and Kooiman's daughter, Pat, immediately volunteered for baby-sitting duty. The Kieltys were mildly taken aback by the rural atmosphere, a major departure from city life. Barb Kielty quipped that while she didn't feel she had reached the end of the world, she swears

Roosevelt Coach C. Wayne Courtney and Senior Ken Kielty discuss strategy of Teddies' next basketball game in 1949.

Elmer Kooiman driving his classic car in the Dutch Festival Parade with passenger Dan Kielty.

Thelma Kooiman's specialty, a sour cream raisin pie.

that she could see it from her front steps. But once she joined the morning coffee circle, she felt extremely comfortable in her new surroundings.

Kielty had little time to assess his surroundings. He assisted in football with the Flying Dutchmen only a couple weeks away from their opener, and although he had an extensive background in football, he had an eleven-man background and needed a crash course in the six-man version.

"It was weird," Kielty said. "You had no tackles or guards and if you didn't have a highly athletic back, you weren't going to score enough to win. But Bill and I worked well together. He was a very good coach and I learned. We got the job done . . . had a very good season."

Once the 5 and 0 with 1 tie football season was over, Kielty and Standly began preparing for the basket-

In the fall of 1955, Barb and Ken Kielty with son, Dan, and baby daughter, Theresa.

Dan and Theresa are ready to ride with Kooimans in the 1958 Dutch Festival Parade.

ball season, Standly began his varsity season with a relatively experienced team, but Kielty was greeted by a "B" team that included nine seventh and eighth graders among his sixteen-man squad. Kielty gave the older players the majority of "B" squad time, preparing them for eventual varsity play, but he recognized the younger players' potential and organized a weekend developmental program that included Dean Veenhof, Darrell Kreun, LeRoy Graphenteen, and several others who, four years later, would help shape the legend that was Edgerton basketball. The emphasis the first season was primarily fundamentals and drills that he learned from Courtney at Roosevelt, but the second season he added an abbreviated schedule against the Christian School and several nearby communities, including Luverne.

The 1955-1956 B-Squad (later 1960 State Champions). Left to right: LeRoy Graphenteen, Norm Fey, Dean Verdoes, Daryl Stevens, Dean Veenhof, Glen Groen, Bert Van Hulzen, Bob Wiarda, Ken Kielty, Merlin Menning, Adrian Wolbrink, Clarence Tinklenberg, Dale Strassburg, Ron Kindt, Ollie Enger, Lloyd Zwart, Darrell Kreun; in front Judy Zwart, Jan Beukelman, and Bev Schoolmeester.

He was the varsity coach the second season and, despite a heavier workload in school, he expanded the program, but he received support from another coach, veteran Harry Franz, a prominent southern Minnesota basketball figure who played on Mountain Lake's 1939 state championship team, a South Dakota State starter, and varsity basketball coach at Luverne from 1947 until sidelined by a heart attack before the 1957-1958 season. Franz introduced the relative newcomer, Kielty, to area coaches and helped him organize a larger schedule highlighted by lengthy scrimmages against Luverne, home and away.

"Harry was an excellent coach, and I enjoyed my time with him," Kielty said. "He and I talked many times about District 8 basketball . . . past, present, and future. We played four games against Luverne—two at each place—

and we let the kids play all day. Harry, too, recognized the potential of the Edgerton kids."

Not that the junior program meant more basketball for the Edgerton youngsters. If they hadn't been playing organized basketball on Saturdays, they'd have been playing at one of several outdoor courts. Pickup basketball at anytime of the year was a way of life in Edgerton. They'd flock to the tiny Edgerton public gym whenever possible, but the next most popular court was in the alley between the Kooiman house and the Huisken grocery. In the autumn, the youngsters would play basketball while listening to Gopher football games on the radio. In the summer, they'd play baseball in the mornings and afternoon, but before nightfall they would be assembled somewhere playing three-on-three games, horse, or simply shooting the ball. When the older boys came up a player or two short for a pickup game, they would recruit grade-school observers such as Vernon Schoolmeester and Jake Kooiman, prominent members of Edgerton basketball in the early to mid-1960s.

"Kids today have played one hundred games by eighth grade," Dean Verdoes said. "But we played as much back then as the kids do today . . . we just played amongst ourselves. There were no boundaries, where one group didn't associate with another. Everybody knew one another and wanted to play."

Standly guided the 1955-1956 Edgerton varsity team to a 13 and 9 season that included a pair of tournament victories before losing to eventual district champion Luverne. As Standly suggested the previous summer, he resigned that spring to accept a teaching and assistant coaching job at Albert Lea. Kielty then got the varsity job and a bonus. The Edgerton school board decided to split varsity football and basketball coaching assignments, and superintendent C.H. Gibson hired Arlie Steen, who had been successful at three South Dakota high schools, to coach varsity football and "B" squad basketball.

"Ken was a hard, hard worker," Steen said. "He spent an awful lot of time working with the program. Rich [Olson] did a great job with that [1960] championship team, but he didn't have a great deal of building to do when he got there. Ken spent so much time working with those kids."

Kielty began his first varsity season with one returning starter, Joe Brouwer. The younger players were not ready for varsity play, and the starting lineup was Brouwer, Harris Tinklenberg, Larry Thorson, Duane Landhuis, and junior Glen Schelhaas, who because of his respect for his summer baseball coach, Kielty, transferred over from the Christian School that fall. The Flying Dutchmen hung around the .500 mark through much of the season, but, hindered by a lack of depth, they lost their last five games and finished 9 and 11 after being eliminated by Ellsworth in the district tournament. Brouwer was Edgerton's leading scorer in almost every game and closed with a 310 point total, but he graduated that spring and Kielty was faced with an even greater challenge the next season.

"For the first time, the Christian School impact really became apparent," Kielty said. "There was a definite shift in talent."

In the six years since the Christian School adopted a four-year high-school curriculum, its enrollment consistently increased, and by the fall of 1956 it had 156 students compared to Edgerton's 100. Coach Melvin DeGroot's Eagles basketball team finished the season 15 and 6 and although Southwest Christian played a softer schedule, the Flying Dutchmen certainly would have avoided a losing season with

Myron Vander Pol (332 points), Ervin Walhof (202), George Huisken (201), or any combination of the three.

"We just didn't have enough support for Brouwer," Kielty said. "But some good things did happen. Arlie Steen did an excellent job with the "B" team. Some of his players received varsity time and younger players Veenhof, Kreun, and Graphenteen continued to benefit from the Saturday practices and games, particularly those against Luverne."

Steen's "B" squad finished 13 and 6, winning eleven of its last twelve games, led by freshmen: Dean Verdoes with 180 points, Bob Wiarda 139 and Lloyd Zwart 88.

At the beginning of the 1957-1958 school year, the starting lineup was three seniors, one junior, and one sophomore. In a preseason article, the *Enterprise* wrote, "Fans will be seeing many new faces this season," and that proved to be an understatement. Early on, a frustrated Kielty called some of his older players aside and told them that he was going to launch a youth movement, promising only that he'd play them whenever possible.

This didn't immediately solve the second-year head coach's problems. For the season, ten different players, a handful called up from the "B" squad, received starts in an assortment of lineups.

"Bill Fure came up to me one day and asked me when I was going to settle on the starting five," Kielty said of the first-year school superintendent who had coached at Chatfield before coming to Edgerton. "I told him that I didn't know if I was ever going to find one, and I really never did." Edgerton finished 8 and 12, the final victory secured in a consolation game against Lake Wilson after the Dutchmen were eliminated by Ellsworth. In retrospect, the season should have been assessed as a turning point and not a low point in Edgerton basketball. The starting lineup at seasons end was one senior, one junior, two sophomores, and 6-foot-4 freshman center Dean Veenhof.

At a time when New Prague's Ron Johnson, Bemidji's Ray Cronk, and Belview's Jon Hagen were capturing the state's fancy, Veenhof made his varsity debut and launched his ascent to all-state status. The left-handed Veenhof came off the bench in Edgerton's opener and scored four points, but started the second game against Lake Wilson and scored twenty-two. He missed only one game in his four-year varsity career, finishing with a school-record 1,887 points and a host of rebounds, a statistic that along with assists didn't become popular until a few years later. Meanwhile, the "B" team finished 16 and 2 and outscored the opposition 700 to 367. Some of that team's stars would join Veenhof in Edgerton's turnaround season.

The townspeople had been patient during Edgerton's two losing seasons, Kielty emphasized, and they would be rewarded.

"I wasn't sure how far away we were from becoming a very good team, but I knew that we were coming fast," Kielty said of what would be a 17 and 5 season. "I was extremely confident that we would be capable of beating almost everyone on the next season's schedule . . . the exceptions being Ellsworth, Jasper, and Luverne."

Of Edgerton's twelve losses in 1957-1958, the Flying Dutchmen were winless in three games against Ellsworth, two games against Jasper, and once to Luverne, which—led by George McKay and Larry Rapp—went on to claim its third consecutive District 8 title and reach the Region II regional championship game before losing a 60 to 59 heartbreaker to Mankato. Luverne, seldom forced to rebuild, had Rapp coming back and sophomore Andy Hagemann, a future Cardinals great, coming on strong.

EDGERTON

Dean Veenhof, Harvey Eernisse, and Bob Wiarda were the principle varsity returnees in the late fall of 1958, having finished first, second, and fourth in scoring. Also returning from the varsity squad came a cadre of promising players led by Dean Verdoes, Darrell Kreun, Barney Van Essen, Daryl Stevens, Norman Fey, and Lloyd Zwart. Left back on the "B" squad was LeRoy Graphenteen, the team's leading scorer a year earlier, a decision with which Graphenteen had no quarrel, but years later Kielty expressed his regret.

"I made a mistake by not calling [Graphenteen] up," Kielty said of the guard who once again led the "B" squad scoring with 175 points. "He was not that much over 5 feet tall, but I put too much emphasis on his size and didn't give enough consideration to his many skills and competitive nature. He was an excellent defensive player and he could shoot when he had to."

Several off-season events are worthy of mention. Kielty and his Legion baseball team, including nearly the entire basketball roster, won the sub-district title but withdrew because many of the players' parents refused to play them on the Sabbath. Kielty had better fortune as town team player-manager for Pipestone, which won the 1958 Class B title. Arlie Steen was named Edgerton's principal, replacing longtime administrator J.H. Brovold, who preferred to concentrate on teaching and counseling, and John Rath became the varsity football and "B" team basketball coach.

Just down the street in Edgerton, Bernard DeWitt was named the Christian School's varsity basketball coach, replacing Melvin DeGroot. The Christian School's enrollment was already larger than Edgerton High's and the basketball program was thriving. In DeGroot's last season, forty candidates reported for the first practice.

After the Flying Dutchmen's winless seven-game football season was completed, Kielty eagerly launched his basketball preparation, buoyed by the realization that for the first time he had depth entering the season. In contrast to his second season, when he futilely attempted to find a starting lineup, he quickly settled into a seven-man rotation, making only occasional lineup changes based on matchups. Barney Van Essen began the season as a top reserve, but the rapidly improving senior forward who transferred over from the Christian School two years early, eventually replaced Wiarda who still remained an integral man in the rotation.

Edgerton barged into the 1958-1959 season with a 70 to 33 romp over Adrian. That Edgerton defeated Adrian in its opener was a welcome start, but even more encouraging

The 1958-1959 Edgerton Flying Dutchmen. Front row: Darrell Kreun, Norm Fey, Dean Verdoes, Lloyd Zwart, LeRoy Graphenteen, manager Doug Vander Beek. Back row: Ken Kielty, Barney Van Essen, Harvey Eernisse, Dean Veenhof, Bob Wiarda, and Daryl Stevens.

was the thirty-seven-point margin of victory. Although the Dutchmen led the series 13 and 7 during the fifties, the Dragons defeated Edgerton in the previous season opener and had won four of the last six games. Edgerton also defeated Lake Wilson by fifty-two points, but the victory was sandwiched by a seventeen-point loss to Ellsworth and a four-point setback at Jasper. From that point, however, the Flying Dutchmen soared, winning five in a row, highlighted by a twenty-seven-point victory over Slayton, and after a second loss to Ellsworth they reeled off six consecutive wins—the program's longest winning streak since the 1949-1950 Dutchmen opened with eleven in a row.

"Beating Slayton by twenty-seven points was the turning point of the season. We hadn't beaten them for a long time, and we played extremely well," Kielty said. "We had been improving every game and suddenly the players knew they could beat anyone on our schedule, and that a district championship was possible."

In the week before tournament time, Edgerton lost to a talented Jasper team led by Butch Raymond, one of the region's finest all-around athletes who played town team baseball with Kielty on Pipestone's 1958 Class B champion team, but came right back three nights later to defeat Luverne 63 to 57 on the Cardinals home court. If beating Slayton by twenty-seven points was the turning point in Edgerton's season, defeating Luverne for only the second time in a nine-game series dating back to 1952 represented a quantum leap into the district tournament.

"[Luverne coach] Bob Erdman came up to me after the game and said, 'I don't remember any of your kids making a turnover," Kielty said. "I'm not sure if we didn't have a turnover, but we definitely kept them at a minimum and not one coming down the stretch."

EDGERTON

Edgerton had the area's attention, thanks in large part to fifteen-year-old Veenhof who averaged eighteen points a game, underscored by a forty-one-point effort against Hills, a school-record performance that gave him more than 500 in his brief career, earned him the *Sioux Falls Argus Leader* newspaper's "Ace of the Week" citation, and left him only two points shy of the Tri-County scoring record set by Magnolia's Lloyd Voss earlier in the season against Ellsworth.

Kielty was using seven men on a regular basis, led by Veenhof. Kreun, who remembers shooting every day since he completed his freshman season, had a ten-point average sculpted by his uncanny outside shot and almost flawless free-throw shooting. In a practice, Kreun once hit ninety-six consecutive free throws. Verdoes had perhaps the team's best field-goal average but was the team's floor leader and defensive ace. Eernisse and Wiarda had higher scoring totals than Verdoes, but along with Fey and Van Essen, were relied upon more for defense and rebounding.

Veenhof wasn't the only player being heralded in Edgerton. His team-high total was being matched by the Christian School's Tom Den Ouden who led the 17 and 3 Eagles to a Tri-State Academy League title. With both Edgerton and the Christian School matching win for win, Arlie Steen—Edgerton principal and part-time *Enterprise* sport columnist—remarked that "If [the two] Edgerton teams could combine their teams, I believe we would be going to Williams Arena in March."

Nice thought but strictly fantasy. The two schools scrimmaged occasionally but for several decades declined to play a regulation game. In March 1959, the Christian School completed its Tri-State Academy Championship season at 17 and 3, while the 14 and 4 Edgerton advanced to the District 8 Tournament, looking for a district title and maybe more.

Edgerton began its bid slowly, struggling three periods before pulling away from a Beaver Creek team it had defeated

Jasper's Butch Raymond challenges Edgerton's Dean Verdoes in 1959 district final.

The Dutchmen were dejected after losing District 8 championship game in the last second.

by eighteen and nineteen points in Tri-County play. Veenhof was held to six points, but Van Essen stepped up with a season-high nineteen and Verdoes chipped in with twelve. Ellsworth, 18 and 1, came next and when Veenhof drew his fourth foul midway through the third quarter, the Panthers appeared headed for a third consecutive victory over the Dutchmen. But Kielty stuck with Veenhof to the end and his twenty-nine points were the foundation of a 62 to 59 upset.

"I told him that we couldn't win without him . . . that I didn't want him to even touch anyone," Kielty said.

Flying Dutchmen captain Harvey Eernisse accepts the District 8 runner-up trophy.

"Ellsworth was probably the best team in the district; in fact, the coach was fired right there on the court. It really was embarrassing.

"We were standing there conversing and someone came up and told him he was fired. I asked him, 'who was that?' He said 'that was the chairman of the school board. He's disliked me for a long time.'"

Fulda added an upset of its own, eliminating three-time defending district champion Luverne. Edgerton defeated Fulda in the next round, and Jasper was all that stood between Edgerton and a Region II berth.

"I really thought we were going to win it all," Kielty said, and the Flying Dutchmen came within seconds of doing so. They led by a point with thirty-one seconds left, but Edgerton let it slip away with a late turnover and a missed free throw, and Jim Cragoe's desperation shot fell to complete a 65 to 64 victory for Jasper.

"It was a very long trip from Worthington to Edgerton that night," Kielty said. "When we got back we held a team meeting and discussed what the team and each individual had to work on to become better and more decisive. It was one of several opportunities Edgerton had to win a district championship and again we let it get away."

The next morning, Fure was in his office and heard a ball bouncing in the gym. When he entered he saw the left-handed Veenhof working with his right hand in preparation for his junior season. For Edgerton players, the season ended Friday night in the disheartening loss to Jasper, but Saturday morning they already were beginning a wondrous journey, but one that Ken Kielty would observe from afar.

CHAPTER FOUR
A Change in Command

Richie Olson was taking postgraduate classes and working at a Bloomington bowling alley when Ken Kielty resigned from Edgerton High School in the spring of 1959.

Olson had never heard of Edgerton, Superintendent Bill Fure, and knew nothing about the southwest Minnesota town, but less then a month after meeting Fure, the former Macalester College standout was directing the town's summer recreation program and playing pickup basketball with some of the players who would share in a fairytale season. Not that Fure had welcomed Kielty's resignation. He was superintendent with a basketball background, a former Luther College athlete who, before moving to Edgerton, taught and coached eight years at Chatfield near Rochester, six basketball seasons, including 1948-1949, when his team won the District 1 title and lost to Rochester, the eventual Region I champion who placed third in the state. Fure was delighted with the Flying

Dutchmen's season, the school's best since 1950, and he urged the school board to give Kielty a $400 raise. When he arrived, Kielty figured that he would stay no longer than two or three years, but he and his wife were comfortable in the rural setting, and he wanted a chance to help secure a district title that had eluded Edgerton for forty years.

Kielty, however, also was the father of three and struggling to make ends meet. He no longer had a Pipestone town team baseball salary to supplement his income, and Barb was a stay-at-home mother of three preschoolers at a time when day care wasn't an option. Edgerton High's math teacher didn't have to do the math to consider his situation negotiable, knowing that he could nearly double his salary in the Minneapolis school system. When the school board rejected his request for a raise, Kielty resigned, and Fure was forced to launch a job search.

Fure quickly established a short list and was prepared to hire a candidate with coaching experience, but placed his decision in abeyance until after a recruiting trip to several Twin Cities colleges. At Macalester, Fure noticed Olson's name and was impressed by his athletic

Rich Olson takes a break from work to bowl a game.

credentials, so he called the former Mac star and arranged a meeting at a Bloomington bowling alley where Olson worked part time.

"I already was impressed with his scholastic record because I knew he was in graduate school," Fure said. "We had a fairly lengthy conversation. I was impressed by his maturity for someone so young, and I liked the way he handled people at the bowling alley. He was the kind of guy who took charge. There was some question in Rich's mind about taking the job, but we finally sold him on our situation."

Olson originally had set his sights higher than high school basketball. He had applied for the Macalester basketball job and was led to believe he was a legitimate candidate. He even received an interview, but in retrospect he sensed that the interview was little more than a courtesy gesture. While waiting for the Macalester athletic board's decision, Olson ignored several high school opportunities, and by the time the school announced they had hired Doug Bolstorff, the positions already were filled. He had married the former Marlys Hannay in April, shortly before she graduated from Macalester, and now both were looking for a job.

"I was thinking more and more about going back to where Iron Rangers always go," said Olson, born and raised in the Minnesota's iron ore region. "But Fure kept coming back, and I finally agreed. I don't believe I would have gone there if he hadn't been so persistent."

Fure's decision to hire a twenty-two-year-old with no previous coaching experience may have come as a surprise to some parents and fans of the Flying Dutchmen players. Three of the four coaches who succeeded Brovold were first-year coaches, but all four were military veterans and significantly older. In fact, Olson's boyish appearance made the slender, blond Norwegian appear as if he should be taking high school biology rather than teaching it. The standard joke in his first season was that he drank coffee rather than milk to let people know who was the coach.

In fairness to Olson—who turned twenty-three that December—although he was young and had no coaching experience, he had a keen basketball mind. There were no guarantees that an outstanding player would be an exemplary coach, but Olson possessed a high basketball intelligence quotient. Long before he arrived in Edgerton . . . even long before he left the Iron Range for Macalester College, he had been preparing to become a coach. His passion for basketball stretched back to his early grade-school days when he would sneak onto the Gilbert team bus. He simply didn't watch high school games, he analyzed them in a manner beyond his years.

"Ever since I can remember, I've been interested in basketball," Olson told a reporter during Edgerton's 1960 state tournament run. "Every Christmas, the family gift would be a new basketball. I had a pretty strong knowledge of the game by my junior or senior year in high school, and around the tenth or eleventh grade I pretty much knew that I wanted to be a coach.

"People would ask me, 'You don't really want to be a coach, do you?' but I did. At that time coaches were respected far more than they are today."

Olson lived in Gilbert through the sixth grade and was one of the Buccaneers' major fans in a town where basketball and not hockey was the winter sport of choice. He avidly followed Gilbert's 1951 state champion team led by future Gopher Bill Simonovich, a 6-foot-10 center, and 6-foot-3 Tom Richardson. But even before Gilbert became one of Minnesota's heralded small-town Cinderella stories, Olson was smitten by Buccaneers basketball. One of his older brothers, Floyd, was captain of the Buccaneers, who won the 1948 District 27 championship before losing to Hibbing in the regional tournament. Floyd, called Govie, also played on a Virginia Junior College team that qualified for the national tournament and was recruited by Macalester where he was captain of the 1952 Scots.

One of Olson's major training grounds was the dirt court behind his home in Virginia, Minnesota, perched on the periphery of the Mountain Iron School District. The Olson boys and their father, Ragnar, a Norwegian immigrant from Oslo who was a railroad engineer for the Duluth-Winnipeg-Pacific line, dug out a basement under their Mountain Iron home, then spread and tamped the loamy soil into a level court. A sand-sheet backboard with a rim intentionally welded a couple inches smaller than regulation was attached to the garage. The smaller rim may have had something to do with the sparkling field-goal and free-throw percentages Olson compiled throughout his high school and college days.

Rich Olson and brother Govie discuss strategy.

David Schley, four years younger than Rich and one of his greatest fans, lived across the street from the Olson house and, years later, vividly recalled the family's backyard games played year around, sometimes going late into the evening through the use of a light attached to a long extension cord. Games were extremely physical—sometimes even a little bloody—and frequently got so loud that neighbors complained.

"Rich was one of the youngest so he often got the crap beat out of him, so he had to be tough," Schley said. "Rich always seemed to have a basketball in his hand and he'd come over to the house and get me to rebound for him when he wasn't playing a game. I thought he was great and watched him play basketball in junior college. He was built kind of gangly, a little like [late Louisiana State University great] Pete Maravich, and he was a gunner. I don't think I've ever met a more competitive person, whether it was in basketball, marbles, or whatever."

The Olsons then moved from Gilbert to West Virginia, a Virginia, Minnesota, suburb in the Mountain Iron School District where Ragnar could be closer to his work. Rich Olson left behind friends who would later play for highly competitive Buccaneer teams, but Mountain Iron also took basketball seriously. He was barely 5 feet when he began junior high, but the kid who, according to his brother Bob, broke an

Rich Olson's brother Ralph, mother, Alice, and father, Ragnor, stand on the backyard court, which was always busy.

arm a couple times climbing trees, channeled that kinetic childhood energy into an intense athletic drive. He played "B" team ball in ninth grade, and as a 5-foot-5 sophomore made the Mountain Iron varsity tournament team, which reached the District 27 semifinals before losing to Virginia, an eventual state tournament qualifier that lost a first-round heartbreaker to Halstad. Mountain Iron was coached by Reuben Epp, a former all-state player at Mountain Lake in southern Minnesota.

"We were leading by five points in the fourth quarter, but we turned the ball over a few times and missed some key free throws in the last couple minutes," Rich's brother Bob, a senior starter, said of a 46 to 44 loss to Virginia. "One guy on our team missed seventeen free throws, and the team missed twenty-three overall. I was ill and didn't start for the first time in three seasons, but eventually the assistant coach convinced the coach to put me in.

"I'm sure Rich was really itching to get into that game, too. He was probably the most competitive member of our family."

Although Bob and Rich Olson were only two years apart and played ball together at Mountain Iron, Rich cited his brother Floyd and Virginia Junior College coach Bill Monat for having the greatest influence on his basketball. Floyd Olson entered the service after leaving Macalester and, after his discharge, embarked on a long-time coaching career at Cook, a town north of Virginia.

Olson said, "I learned most of my basketball from my brother, Govie,

Bill Monat, Virginia J.C. coach, taught Rich Olson much of his basketball knowledge and skills.

Rich protects the ball while at Virginia J.C.

and Monat. Govie taught me how to shoot the jump shot, and I had never cared much for defense until Monat pointed out how important it was . . . showing me what to do in a man-to-man to stop some of those NJCC stars."

Olson's two seasons as a Mountain Iron starter were forgettable, though he played well enough to attract some attention from college coaches. But he had five other brothers and two sisters, and the scholarship offers weren't enough to cover his expenses, and his parents weren't able to help out so he enrolled at Virginia Junior College. He paid minimal tuition, lived within walking distance from school, and worked part time in the community recreation center, where he had the opportunity to increase his practice time. Besides, what was good enough for Floyd, who played two years for Virginia JC and won a junior college national tournament season, was good enough for little brother.

Olson also played two seasons for Monat, one of the Iron Range's most respected coaches, and in his second season he was named to the first-team all-Northern Junior College Conference team. The 5-foot-11 senior forward led the conference in scoring with a school-record 395 points, finished third on his team with eighty-seven rebounds, made sixty-four assists, and defensively created far more turnovers than he committed, but spoke more fondly of his first season at Virginia JC.

EDGERTON

"We probably should have gone all the way to the nationals that year," Olson said. "We had a very good center, but he was more interested in becoming a doctor than in basketball; in fact, he did become a doctor. We needed more out of him to get over the hump."

Olson's second season wasn't one of Monat's finest, either, but the coach who, in more than twenty-five seasons, produced many outstanding NAIA and NCAA players was exceptionally proud of Olson, describing him as the "best shot I've ever coached" after a season which, in sixteen games, Olson broke the school single-season scoring record that had been established in twenty-five games. When Monat retired in 1957, he sent a form letter to his former players, but added a handwritten postscript to Olson, commending him for his dedication and determination. "You won many games for our team, Rich," Monat concluded. "Keep up the good work this year and apply the same attitude and desire in life. Nothing comes easy, but you got the stuff to come through."

Once again, Olson attracted recruiting attention from colleges as far away as Florida State, but he chose to follow in Floyd's footsteps at Macalester. Olson received full tuition, earned his room and board working in the field house and the women's dorm, which he opened in the morning and locked at night. His only personal expense was spending money.

Olson started immediately at Macalester, scoring twenty-two points in the first game ever played in the college's new field house, and received all-Minnesota Interscholastic Conference honorable mention in a 13 to 10 season. He also received the annual "M" Award, which went to the Scot letterman with the highest academic average. As a senior, he led the team in scoring and was the national NAIA scoring leader until late January when he sprained an ankle. The injury slowed his pace, and he also lost his lead in the conference scoring race, but he played well enough to become the team's leading scorer and earn first-team status on the *St. Paul Pioneer Press-Dispatch* all-MIAC team.

A photo caption in Macalester's 1958 yearbook read: "Olson's favorite shot was the turnaround jump shot, which he scored with remarkable consistency, even though he usually was guarded by players several inches taller than he."

Olson uses his trademark jump shot while playing for Macalester College.

What Olson didn't learn about the game from "Govie" and Monat, he discovered through the role he played in the Macalester offense. He began a possession taking the ball up-court as a guard, but moved into a forward slot once he crossed the midcourt line. In addition to his basketball knowledge, Olson was extremely athletic. He also lettered in baseball and track both seasons, winning the 1958 MIAC pole vault after making an eleventh-hour decision to compete.

Macalester basketball was coached by Dwight Stuessy when Olson enrolled, but during his junior season Stuessy died of a heart attack after the Scots defeated cross-town rival St. Thomas in a hard-fought game. "We were trailing at halftime, but we came back to win, and I finished with twenty-two points," Olson said. "[Stuessy] came up to me in the locker room, told me I had an outstanding game and gave me a hug. Then, he walked around to the other side of the lockers and collapsed."

Ralph Lundeen became the Scots' interim coach until Gil Wilson was hired, but after the 1957-1958 season he resigned to become a businessman. About the time Olson learned that he was not going to be the next Macalester coach, Fure arrived in the area and wound up interviewing Olson for a coaching position that was virtually filled when he left Edgerton. He was impressed by Olson but the candidate wasn't particularly overwhelmed by the prospects of teaching biology and physical education and coaching three sports in a small southwestern Minnesota town, far from both the Twin Cities and the Iron Range. Fure, however, eventually convinced Olson to accept his offer, and control of Flying Dutchmen basketball was in the hands of an intense and precocious first-year coach.

Rich Olson sits in on a class taught by his wife, Marlys, but his mind was obviously elsewhere. The Dutchman won the Region Two title on the eve of his wife's birthday, and her husband was preparing for Edgerton's state tournament title bid.

Olson's decision was based on scant options, but he was offered several attractive incentives. This was a chance to run his own program, rather than begin as an assistant in a larger school. He was appointed the town's summer recreation director, earning him an extra $400. And in addition to his teaching and coaching salary, his recent bride, a Macalester graduate, Marlys, was promised a job in Edgerton's elementary school, not far from her home town in Amboy.

By mid-June his days were spent directing the community's recreation program, coaching the American Legion and youth teams, and driving a busload of children to Pipestone twice a week for swimming lessons. In the evening, he began playing pickup games with some of the returning Flying Dutchmen players . . . not unlike his pickup days behind his house in Mountain Iron.

"I thought, 'Holy cow, they're too small to be good,'" Olson said of initial reaction to the players. "Wiarda was the only one of them with any girth. I wondered how the people in town thought those kids could play. My thoughts of winning our district or regional tournament were somewhat remote."

What Olson didn't realize immediately was that basketball was as important to the players as it was to him; in fact their upbringing wasn't that much different than his. In an era of economic growth, which had not been manifested in small-town life, jobs weren't that plentiful for kids, and that was wonderful for the closely knit youngsters who spent countless hours playing basketball from the time they were in grade school. Even some farm kids such as Veenhof and Wiarda enjoyed it so much that they found ways to get to town before or after their chores.

"My dad let me drive the tractor to town until I was old enough to get a driver's license," Veenhof said. "That worked out pretty well because they were able to drag the infield for baseball, too."

Olson knew the team won seventeen games the previous season, but he was an Iron Range native who knew little about the area, so he had no point of reference to compare their previous season's accomplishment to ability. The

Dutchmen had beaten larger schools Slayton and Luverne, but Olson didn't have film to determine their competitive level. Ellsworth was 18 and 1 when defeated by Edgerton in the district semifinals, but it might have been a fluke considering that Ellsworth defeated the Dutchmen twice during the regular season. And finally, he knew they lost to Jasper, another small town, in the district tournament but he knew nothing about Jasper's Butch Raymond, one of the best all-around athletes in southwest Minnesota.

Farm kids used different modes of travel into town.

What he had to recognize was the Edgerton players' steely resolve, derived from the bitter loss to Jasper when they were within a heartbeat of a regional berth. The Flying Dutchmen owned a three-point lead with less than a minute remaining, but let it get away with Veenhof and Kreun on the bench, the high-scoring center picking up his fifth foul with six minutes left, and Kreun picking up his fifth two minutes later. Still, they might have won if not for Raymond's stellar play, a couple late fouls, and Jim Cragoe's desperation game-winning shot with three seconds left.

"The Jasper game was especially painful for me because I missed a free throw late in the game," Verdoes said. "The ball hit between the rim, started falling in but bounced out. I don't know why it didn't fall.

"I think I shed tears for at least a week, but as painful as the loss was to us, everyone knew that we had become a competitive team, and we knew that we'd have a good team the next year."

Against the backdrop of the previous season, optimism would indeed abound within the team and the community heading into the new school year. No one could imagine how good they would be, but certainly a district championship—something no Flying Dutchmen basketball team had ever attained—was a distinct possibility. Establishing a goal to win or even reach the state tournament, however, might have been considered inflated ambition. No District 8 representative had reached the state tournament since Luverne in 1938 and no Region II champion had won a state title since Mountain Lake in 1939.

No matter how far the players expected to go the next season, when they recovered from the Jasper loss, they assumed Kielty would lead them until his resignation was announced in mid-May. They were disappointed to see him go and more than a trifle curious as to why he'd want to leave. Edgerton lost only Barney Van Essen and Harvey Eernisse, journeyman players, and they had Graphenteen and Jim Roos, promising players, coming up from a "B" team that finished 16 to 2. Graphenteen sprouted a couple of inches to 5-foot-8 and had a good chance to start at guard, allowing the 6-foot-3 Verdoes to become a forward. And Roos—although relatively new to the Flying Dutchmen program—had enough athletic talent to warrant quality playing time.

But one major characteristic defined the Flying Dutchmen cast, "focus." They quickly acquired a strong bond with their new coach and adjusted to his intense coaching style. And what was not to like about Olson? He was a former college star with uncanny accuracy, a passion for basketball and a profound knowledge of the game, and he was willing to spend hours playing pickup alley ball with a bunch of teens.

Veenhof recalled the many evenings when Kreun, Graphenteen, and he would go three-on-three against Verdoes, Wiarda, and the coach. Olson cut them no slack in the games, competing as fiercely as he did in his high school and college days, but he also was assessing the personnel and how each might fit into an offense he had been sculpting since his Mountain Iron days.

"I never read a coaching book until much later in my career when I read one of [UCLA legend] John Wooden's, but I knew exactly what I wanted to do," Olson said referring to the UCLA legend. "I came here with my offense written down on one sheet of paper. I made some changes and had a pretty good idea what my starting lineup would be before the season began.

"They never got tired of playing. My wife got the biggest kick out of the day when Darrell Kreun came to the house with a basketball under his arm and asked if the coach could come out and play."

Inquiring minds might ask what would have happened had the Edgerton school board granted Kielty the $400 raise or if he had stayed despite the rejection. What if Olson had accepted another job immediately out of college and not come to Edgerton? Would the Flying Dutchmen have gone as far with Kielty or possibly another coach? Fure chooses not to speculate. Instead he simply implies that Kielty conditioned the players to believe they could win and Olson pushed them hard to build on that belief.

"Richie's hiring was solid. I wanted someone who was strong and knew the game, and Richie was strong and knew the game." he said. "Although he scared me at times, I've always said that Olson was the right man for the job, but that Ken Kielty really worked hard with the kids and spent a lot of time with them."

The players have remained close to both coaches far beyond their high-school days. They always have expressed a profound appreciation for both men who prepared them for their incredible journey but avoid comparisons like technical fouls. Verdoes, a longtime fishing buddy of Kielty's and an Olson admirer, offers an introspective response when asked how Edgerton might have fared with Kielty as the coach.

"I'm about an eight-handicap in golf, and yesterday I shot a 71," he began. "If you asked me if I'm going to shoot a 71 tomorrow, I'd say probably not . . . but who knows. You need a multitude of things to happen for [a state championship]. Our story could have ended in Mountain Lake [1960 regional final] . . . or even in Pipestone [1960 district semifinal].

"We had a lot of luck, a lot of good things happen. If Ken had been here, we might have won . . . maybe not. It's moot. You just have to be glad to have had both those guys as coaches. That's the key. Basketball is a hard game to play and one of the hardest games to coach."

Few players and coaches would ever claim that good things come easy, but a first-year coach and a ragtag bunch of kids from the country made it almost look as if it was effortless in one of the state's most unforgettable seasons in high school basketball, a season that made two coaches and a community proud.

CHAPTER FIVE
The Regular Season

In Edgerton, just like other small towns into the sixties, there was a sport or sports for each season, so Flying Dutchmen athletes played high school baseball or competed in track during the spring, American Legion baseball in the summer, and turned to football when school resumed in the fall. The difference in Edgerton compared with many other small towns in the state was that basketball was played twelve months a year at some level, either pickup games, horse, or simply shooting around.

"We thought of basketball all the time and played almost every day," Dean Veenhof said. "I'd bet out of the 365 days in a year we'd play 345 of them. We'd play American Legion in the summer, but couldn't wait until we got to Kooiman's garage. In the fall, after football we'd play basketball. I can't remember who, but someone had a key to the gymnasium door, and we'd go in and shoot.

"We'd even go in there on Sundays. Nobody knew we were in there. When we got done, we'd put the balls away

Elmer Kooiman built a popular outdoor court, well used by Edgerton's champions.

and lock the door when we went out. I don't remember any talk about the state tournament or how many games we would win. We just wanted to play basketball."

On his opening day as a head coach, Rich Olson greeted twenty-three players, a group led by four returning starters, three other lettermen, and a couple of excellent prospects from the previous season's "B" squad. Olson's practices were long, demanding, and physical, according to several players. He chided them. He scolded them. He challenged them. He granted the reserves physical liberties in defending the starters that occasionally sparked shoving matches and other minor altercations, but his philosophy worked without disrupting team harmony.

"He was a brilliant coach, way ahead of his time," Dean Verdoes said, "and he knew how to handle kids. It's never easy for any first-year coach, I learned that when I began coaching, but it was far, far easier for him because we got to know him that summer and we were a bunch of solid citizens willing to go with the flow."

But as long as Olson's practices went, players voluntarily made them longer by staying late and practicing their conditioning and offense and defensive skills. Olson, too, stuck around to provide some individual instruction or to simply work on his own game for the area's independent town team season. Among the frequent late-afternoon features were the games of horse played between Olson and Kreun, contests in which each demonstrated remarkable marksmanship.

"The games would go on forever. No one would miss," Veenhof said. "They'd be shooting jump shots from

Team manager Doug Vander Beek, the man for all seasons, made a coach's job easier.

twenty, thirty feet and sometimes there would be eighteen, nineteen shots before one of them would miss."

Opening day was November 20 when Edgerton traveled to Adrian, nineteen miles due south in Nobles County, for a Tri-County League game. The two were among 488 schools participating in the Minnesota State High School League basketball season, annually culminated in an eight-team state championship every March in Williams Arena.

To provide a time frame, the game was played on a day when seven European countries formed a free-trade agreement. India proposed mutual withdrawal of Indian and Chinese forces from disputed border areas, including Tibet. Nationally, Alabama Governor John Patterson signed legislation designed to curb Negro voter registration in his state. The U.S. space commission launched Discoverer VIII into a polar orbit from Vandenberg Air Force Base in California, and Allen Freed was fired for payola scandal involving pop music at a time when teens were dancing and humming to hits such as Bobby Darin's "Mack the Knife," Ricky Nelson's "It's Late," and Johnny and the Hurricanes's instrumental "Red River Rock."

Ben Hur just had been released in the movie theaters. Television, which earlier in the decade began to replace radio as the major nighttime entertainment, had recently added *The Untouchables, The Twilight Zone,* and *Dennis the Menace* to the week-night lineup. And in sports, the NBA Minneapolis Lakers were completing a twelve-year run in the Twin Cities, Joe Foss, former South Dakota governor and World War II hero, was pondering an offer to become the first American Football League commissioner (which he accepted), and wheels were in motion to bring major league baseball and NFL football to Minnesota.

Gas was twenty-five cents a gallon, postage four cents, the national average annual income was approximately $3,000, and minimum wage was $1.01 per hour. In Edgerton one certainly couldn't have found more than a handful of town partisans willing to bet on the Dutchmen's chances of a District 8 title that had eluded them too many times in the past, let alone them claiming the state's most coveted high school championship trophy. In the thirteen-team district, most of them representing sparsely populated towns, Luverne and Pipestone—two of the district's largest schools—were the preseason favorites, and one of them was expected to challenge Mankato or Mountain Lake for the Region II title. Wayzata lost nearly everyone from its 1959 championship team, but Region V always had at least a half dozen contenders and had produced state champions in six of the last eight seasons. In the 1958 Region V Tournament, the four district champions were combined 88 and 2 entering the competition.

But, Veenhof emphasized, the Flying Dutchmen were disconnected from any distractions beyond the opening tip-off at Adrian that November day.

"We knew we were good. We played well together," he said, "but we were just a bunch of unassuming, naive country boys playing basketball. That's all we wanted to do. I don't remember any talk about a state championship before the season began or while we went through the season."

Veenhof was the centerpiece of the Edgerton team, a 6-foot-5 junior center who made his first varsity start in the second game of his freshman season. As a freshman and sophomore, he was the team's scoring leader and with 634 career points was the program's most prolific scorer since John Fransen in the mid-fifties. The nephew of Nick

Veenhof, a former Dutchman player, gained regional attention in his sophomore year when he was cited as the *Sioux Falls Argus-Leader*'s "Ace of the Week," and he was beginning to receive some attention at the state level because of his scoring and rebounding. The slender junior was a left-hander with a soft, curling hook shot that he learned from a book Kielty gave him in his freshman season. He also had an effective move underneath that frequently produced easy lay-ups, a move that he enhanced by working with his right hand between his sophomore and junior seasons. His scoring ability was even more impressive, when one considered the time he missed after fouling out or after being forced to sit out because of early foul problems.

Dean Verdoes was a 6-foot-3 forward with a skinny frame and pale complexion, which gave him a fragile look, and he would turn beet red in the up-tempo games, prompting some observers to question his health. The senior team captain, however, was a thirty-two-minute player and an extremely durable athlete who frequently received the toughest defensive assignment inside because of his moxie. He was a high-percentage shooter who could hit that ten- to twelve-foot jumper, and as a junior won the Tri-County League trophy for the highest free-throw percentage, but he generally sacrificed scoring to be a playmaker, working the ball inside to Veenhof or kicking the ball back out to Kreun when Veenhof was lost in a crowd of defenders. In pressure situations, the versatile Verdoes was the go-to player, tall enough to read the floor and poised enough to get the ball in the right hands after making the in-bounds pass. In addition to being a leader on the court, he was one of the school's outstanding students and president of his senior class.

Darrell Kreun was the perfect complement to Veenhof, his deft touch from the outside denying opposing teams to pack it in on the Dutchman center. Kreun, a 5-foot-8 guard, seemed to have no limit to his shooting range and some speculated that in the three-point era he would have fashioned an infinitely higher scoring average. Many of his points, however, came from the free-throw line from where he rarely missed in games, and once in practice sank ninety-six consecutive shots. Kreun had two brothers, Duane and Ron, who played at Edgerton before him and from the moment he saw Duane on Edgerton's tiny court, basketball became his passion. Although quiet, he was intensely competitive—an all-around athlete who also played football and baseball—and after the disappointing tournament loss to Jasper, he said he played or practiced almost every day.

LeRoy Graphenteen was the youngest member in what would be Edgerton's sixteen-year history of Graphenteens in basketball, preceded by Clarence, Arnie, and Les. He was barely 5-foot tall when he reached junior high and received only token varsity duty through his sophomore year when he led the "B" team in scoring, but he began his junior season as a 5-foot-8 guard and was penciled in as a varsity starter once Olson recognized his ability. Graphenteen's major role as a junior was two-fold, handling the ball and playing defense, but he was accurate when given a shooting opportunity and particularly lethal from the free-throw line. The derivation of his nickname "Slug" is subject to debate, but was it in stark contrast to his scrappy brand of play?

Bob Wiarda was in and out of the starting lineup as a junior, much to his dismay, but Olson had a profound appreciation for the 6-foot-2 senior's athletic ability, physical strength and unselfish play, describing him as the team's "unsung hero." The muscular forward particularly was effective on the boards and knew how to get the ball inside to Veenhof without forcing the pass, but had more than a handful of double-figure scoring games.

"All five could shoot, that was the main thing," Olson said. "Kreun was such a good shooter that he never had fear of missing a shot no matter where he was. The same goes for Verdoes. The one who shot the least was Graphenteen, but he played a major defensive role, and he played smart.

"Whatever I told them, they did. They each had a role and they played it to the hilt. They didn't complain

The 1959-1960 Edgerton Flying Dutchmen team. Darrell Kreun, Larry Schoolmeester, Norm Muilenburg, Bob Wiarda, Dean Verdoes, Dean Veenhof, Bob Dykstra, Jim Roos, Daryl Stevens, Darwin Fey, LeRoy Graphenteen, Tom Warren, and Coach Rich Olson.

about practices and I was a long-practice coach. They did not question anything. They played well together and got better in each game."

Olson had three key reserves, seniors 5-foot-11 Daryl Stevens, 5-foot-9 Norm Fey, and 6-foot-3 junior Jim Roos.

Lloyd Zwart, a letterman the previous year, did not play his senior year because he was needed to work on his family farm. Stevens was one of the strongest and fastest Flying Dutchmen, a football standout who offered major rebounding support, while Fey was an experienced guard who was almost the Edgerton hero against Jasper when he made a couple of late free throws to give his team a two-point lead. Roos, a 1957-1958 transfer from nearby Hardwick, was an outstanding athlete who played four sports and was improving rapidly in basketball.

Fey's senior season, however, was over shortly after it began. Angered by an Olson order in practice, Fey harshly responded to the no-nonsense coach and was dismissed from the team. Fey said he might have regained his spot with an apology but was too stubborn and Edgerton's limited depth became shallower. "At the time I thought he was wrong, but I couldn't hold anything against him. He was the coach and expected his players to do what they were told," Fey said years later. "I guess it worked well for the team. LeRoy Graphenteen did a better job than I ever could have. I was a lousy shot."

The remaining varsity roster included 5-foot-6 junior guard Tom Warren and 6-foot junior Norm Muilenburg, plus sophomores Darwin Fey, Bob Dykstra, and Larry Schoolmeester who would split time between the varsity and "B" squad before becoming part of the tournament team. Warren saw little quality playing time, but Darrell Kreun was quick to applaud the diminutive guard's contribution to the team. "He was on my hip from the time we left the locker room until we left the floor," Kreun said. "He helped make me a better player. We had a number of other guys who helped maintain the intensity during practices." Daryl Stevens was an effective reserve in games, but also made a major contribution in practice where he frequently challenged Veenhof.

"Daryl was always about defense, and he was strong," Veenhof said. "We'd get into some good old shoving matches, and we'd both get ticked. But after practice it was over . . . forgotten. We all got along. I don't remember any [off-court] fights or arguments."

Any intensity surrounding Edgerton's opener diminished quickly at Adrian, where the Flying Dutchmen jumped to a seventeen-point first-quarter lead and breezed to an 82 to 46 victory. Veenhof led the way with twenty-four points, followed by Kreun's twenty and Verdoes' nineteen. The decisive triumph came as no surprise to the Dutchmen who defeated the Dragons by thirty-seven and forty-one points the season before, but it was a comfortable start after the previous season's bitter finish.

Edgerton started slowly in the second game, with the Dutchmen and Lake Wilson going scoreless through the first three minutes and eleven seconds, but they broke the shutout, and then Lake Wilson's spirit en route to an 84 to 17 romp in which Veenhof scored twenty-eight points, and three others scored in double figures.

Next came what some expected to be the season's first major challenge, a showdown against Ellsworth which had much of the same personnel back from the 1958-1959 season when the Panthers lost only two games including the upset loss to Edgerton in the post season. Early foul problems forced Veenhof to sit much of the game, but he still scored twenty-two points in what was a satisfying 78 to 51 victory observed by a standing-room-only crowd in Edgerton's home gymnasium.

Before the holiday break, Edgerton improved its record to 6 to 0 defeating Hills 73 to 38, Jasper 92 to 44, and

Magnolia 93 to 67 four nights later. The season's start was Edgerton's best since 1948-1949 and the Dutchmen set back-to-back school single-game scoring records in the Jasper and Magnolia victories—eclipsing the mark of eighty-four set a year earlier against Chandler, the first time an Edgerton team had scored eighty or more points.

The Jasper rout wasn't difficult to understand because the Quartsiters lost several key players, the most significant being Butch Raymond, but the Magnolia score was a mild surprise, if for no other reason than the presence of Lloyd Voss. The muscular 6-foot-4, 225-pound center was one of the region's finest athletes who a season earlier scored a Tri-County record forty-one points against a solid Ellsworth team. Voss wound up at the University of Nebraska after high school and after an outstanding college career was drafted by Green Bay and played nine National Football League seasons for the Packers, Pittsburgh Steelers, and Denver Broncos.

Veenhof and Stevens were two Dutchmen players who could attest to Voss's power based on that fall's Edgerton-Magnolia football game. Veenhof recalled being "knocked loony" and Stevens said his football season almost ended in a collision with the Magnolia hulk.

"I called [for a blitz] in a defensive huddle and I hit him behind the line of scrimmage," Stevens said. "But I got knocked silly in the process. I had spasms and was foaming at the mouth. When I woke up I saw a doctor waving two fingers in my face, and I didn't play for the rest of the game. I had a headache for three or four days, and today they would have probably had me undergo a bunch of tests, but I played the next week."

Voss and the Bulldogs won the football game, but not even the powerful center's thirty-one points and Coach

Darrell Kreun, using his perfect stroke, scored a school-record forty-one points against Magnolia. He hit 15 of 19 field-goal attempts and was 11 for 11 from the free-throw line.

Jerrol Conley's bag of defensive strategies were enough to stymie Edgerton's irresistible offense. Kreun dazzled the home crowd with his deft shooting touch, hitting fifteen of nineteen field-goal attempts and sinking eleven of eleven free throws for a career-high and Tri-County record-tying forty-one points before picking up his fifth foul in the fourth quarter. Three other Dutchmen finished in double figures in an effort that carried Olson into the vacation break with a smile and feeling a twinge of excitement.

"They were a good bunch of kids to work with and were improving every game, but we really hadn't played anyone," Olson said. "But, Kreun had that breakout game, Veenhof played well, and I could see that Verdoes could hold his own. When I got home that night, I remember telling my wife, 'I think we have a chance to do something special.'"

At the holiday break, the numbers were certainly special. The Dutchmen were 6 and 0, owned a 502 to 263 scoring advantage, and their smallest margin of victory was twenty-seven points. Further encouraging was the fact that they defeated Ellsworth and Jasper, the only two teams that defeated them the season before. The holiday schedule included practices every day except Sundays and holidays and they scrimmaged against Tracy, a valuable test considering the Scrappers were a solid team that ultimately finished the season 16 and 5 including a 59 to 53 loss to Minneota in the District 9 championship game.

"The biggest thing we got out of that scrimmage was that we learned how to beat a zone press," Olson explained. "I scheduled that scrimmage specifically because I knew they used it and knew that we'd see it along the way. In fact, I hung on to that lesson the rest of my coaching career."

When they returned fifteen days later, the Dutchmen weren't greeted by a zone press, but Beaver Creek gave them a scare with a well-executed control game. The Dutchmen, averaging 83.7 points per game, scored only two points in the first quarter and trailed by seven points at the half. Olson presented a simple solution: Hold the ball until they could get it to Veenhof or had a lay-up, then protect the ball and don't take any foolish shots once they had the lead. The Dutchmen complied in textbook fashion and Edgerton pulled away. Veenhof scored thirty points and Wiarda next with four, matching the remaining starters combined total.

"It was easier to stall in those days because they didn't have the five-second rule," Olson said. "What I told them after that game is that we were fortunate that it happened when it did because they would be prepared and know what to do the next time it happened."

In the next five games, opponents played Edgerton straight up, and the Dutchmen responded in admirable fashion. They defeated Chandler 55 to 35, getting eighteen points from Kreun and sixteen from Veenhof before turning the game over to the reserves four minutes into the third quarter.

Next came a rematch with Ellsworth, whose only loss to date had been to Edgerton. The Bulldogs trailed by only four points after three quarters, but Veenhof avoided foul problems and was around until the end, and LeRoy Graphenteen provided one of the season's stellar defensive efforts in a 70 to 58 victory. Veenhof scored thirty-one points and Graphenteen held Lee Visker to seven points, thirteen points below his season's average.

After fifty consecutive starts, Veenhof sat out the Lake Wilson game because of a mild ankle sprain suffered in practice, but the Dutchmen darted to a sixteen-point first-quarter lead and breezed to a 73 to 48 romp. Kreun, one of four Dutchmen to score in double figures, had a game-high twenty-two points. Magnolia went to a zone and combined with Voss's twenty points to keep things interesting, but Edgerton emerged with its eleventh straight victory because Veenhof scored twenty-five points playing on a sore ankle and Kreun added eighteen.

Veenhof, back to full strength, scored twenty-seven points against Chandler in an 84 to 31 rout, but next came Hills. Edgerton defeated the Bluejays by thirty-five points early in the season, but the Dutchmen were fortunate to escape the tiny Hills gym with a 59 to 55 decision in which they trailed by three points at the half and didn't take the lead until two and one-half minutes remained in the third quarter. Hugo Goehle, a former Luverne star athlete who had become one of the region's most respected coaches in football and basketball and who would be named to the state high school coaches hall of fame, had his team control the game's tempo most of the way, but his guile could not control Veenhof or his team's performance at the free-throw line. Veenhof scored twenty-eight points and Hills hit only nine of twenty free-throw attempts compared to Edgerton's 19-for-27 execution from the line.

"We had a stretch where we weren't playing that well . . . we were struggling a little bit," Verdoes said. "We had beaten them quite badly and when we played them in their gym, they were ready and we weren't. Maybe we coasted a little emotionally . . . not physically because we never played that way.

"I remember playing harder than heck in that game. There was no team meeting or anything like that after that game, but I think it was a wake-up call for us. We were all intuitive individuals and Rich kept us in line. No one really gave us any trouble until the tournament."

When the season began, the Dutchmen and their town were virtually invisible to those outside of the Tri-County area. The *Edgerton Enterprise* reported regularly on the team's progress, and Corky Brace, the *Worthington Globe*'s veteran sports editor, gave the Dutchmen mention. But as the Edgerton winning streak grew, its reputation began to generate attention beyond southwest Minnesota.

John Egan, the *Sioux Falls Argus Leader* sports editor, began to mention Edgerton's success in his columns and frequently used reports from Francis Verdoes, mother of Dean and an *Argus-Leader* stringer. After the 70 to 58 victory over Magnolia, Veenhof was named the *Argus Leader*'s "Ace of the Week," a citation extended to athletes in the newspaper's tri-state readership area of South Dakota, Iowa, and Minnesota.

Word of Edgerton's success reached *Minneapolis Star and Tribune* sportswriter Ted Peterson who, in late January, wrote a lengthy column on Edgerton's winning streak and its prospects in District 8. But to say that Edgerton had attained household status within Minnesota would be an overstatement. Consider that in another *Star-Tribune* high school note, the writer referred to "Dean Beenhoff" and "Dean Berdoes" after defeating Ellsworth.

And the beat went on. Edgerton defeated Jasper, 68 to 52, for the second time, a gratifying sweep against the team that shattered Edgerton's District 8 dream eleven months earlier. The Dutchmen also went over 1,000 points for the season, with Graphenteen—who finished with a season-high ten points—notching the milestone 1,000th point with a free throw, one of thirty-two for Edgerton.

The Dutchmen defeated Adrian 85 to 53 for their fifteenth consecutive win, tying the school's record winning streak. Three nights later they defeated Beaver Creek 89 to 34 to break the record. The Beavers held Edgerton to a season-low thirty-eight points in December, but in this game Edgerton would score twenty points in the first eight minutes and finished with more than eighty points for the seventh time in the season.

In defeating Beaver Creek, Edgerton completed its Tri-County Conference season undefeated and had only two non-conference games remaining in its regular season. They weren't, however, just any two games. They faced Slayton and Luverne, two of the district's bigger schools, with both games on the road. Edgerton defeated both schools a year earlier, but the series records in each case were woeful through the fifties. The Dutchmen were 4 and 10 against the Wildcats and 2 and 7 against the Cardinals, the latter having been added to Edgerton's regular schedule in 1952.

Beyond the dismissal of Fey in the early season and a minor scare when Veenhof sprained his ankle, Edgerton's season had been a relatively smooth journey, free of major incidents and injuries, but on the Monday practice before meeting Slayton, the team experienced a critical setback, one that resonated into the tournament season. Jim Roos, one of Edgerton's top reserves, broke his left arm in practice, and the only veteran Dutchmen reserve remaining was Daryl Stevens.

"I wasn't able to dunk the ball, but I was strong enough to grab the rim," said Roos who wore a cast from his wrist to his forearm. "I grabbed it, and my momentum carried me parallel to the floor. I lost my grip and fell . . . my rear end hurt more than my arm, and I was probably more embarrassed than anything."

Depth was no problem against Slayton; in fact, nine players played and eight of them scored in an 82 to 47 victory in which Veenhof and Verdoes each scored twenty-two points, and guards Kreun and Graphenteen added fifteen points each. The Wildcats trailed by only eight points at the half, but Edgerton scored forty-four points in the second half while Olson emptied his bench.

Luverne and its second-year coach Bob Erdman began the season with many new faces, but the Cardinals always seemed to come up with a competitive team and this season was no exception. Led by Andy Hagemann, Bill Mohr, and Larry Rapp, Luverne was 13-3 heading into the Edgerton game, losing two contests to Pipestone and a two-point decision to Jackson. In addition to the loss of Roos, Olson feared he might have to play without Verdoes who was suffering from the flu.

"I was sick as a dog . . . in bed for two days," Verdoes said. "I probably shouldn't have played and [Superintendent] Bill Fure usually didn't allow you to play if you were sick and missed school, but he said, 'If you can get up, you go for it.' I got to school around noon and I played that night."

Verdoes started and played most of a game in which Olson used only six players in what would be a 76 to 65 victory over the Cardinals. Edgerton quickly claimed the lead in a packed Luverne gymnasium and held it throughout the game. The Dutchmen led by 15 points at the intermission and appeared ready to run away until Veenhof was forced to the bench because of foul problems. The Cardinals closed to within five points before Veenhof returned and Luverne's comeback stalled. Four Dutchmen finished in double figures, Kreun scoring twenty points and Wiarda collecting a season-high nineteen, and Edgerton was an immaculate 30 for 35 in free throws.

Verdoes was held to five free throws, but played an integral role in the victory with his defensive play, his rebounding, and his leadership against Luverne's pesky pressure defense.

"Dutchmen beat Luverne for perfect 18 and 0 season," the *Enterprise* headline screamed that week. The enthusiasm might have even been understated in that from a starting field of 488 schools in the MSHSL, seven were unbeaten, the others being Cloquet, Dodge Center, Duluth Central, Esko, Forest Lake, and Renville. Melrose, Chisholm, and Argyle had only one loss.

The Flying Dutchmen, however, didn't feel as if they were living in a perfect world. They wanted nothing less than a District 8 title, something that had eluded the school since the program was launched in the twenties. But for the first time since they began the streak, they dwelled on the present before refocusing on the future.

"We were undefeated," Kreun said, "and any time we beat Luverne it was a big deal at our school because we didn't beat them that often. I'm sure that some people thought that if there was a game we would lose, it would be to Luverne. But we won, and I'm sure that helped in the tournament."

CHAPTER SIX
The District and Region Tournament

From the regular-season opener at Adrian to the season finale at Luverne, Coach Rich Olson's mantra was "one game at a time," but while the players faithfully complied, he took the liberty of thinking ahead after his team's record-scoring romp over Magnolia just before the fifteen-day holiday break.

"After [the Magnolia game], I began to scout Pipestone whenever I had the opportunity," Olson said. "They were considered one of the best teams in the state, and I figured that we'd have to beat them if we wanted to get out of the district. I probably saw them play five, six, or maybe seven times that season . . . and I scouted Luverne a few times too."

The way the District 8 tournament bracket was structured, Edgerton and Pipestone would meet in the semifinals if they both were fortunate to get that far. The Dutchmen would have to defeat Magnolia and the winner of the Hills and Chandler game in the sub-district, while

94

Pipestone only would have to defeat Luverne, the district champion in three of the last four years but a team the Arrows had defeated twice during their Southwest Conference championship season.

Edgerton was the only unbeaten team in the district and had defeated every District 8 team except Pipestone, Worthington, and Fulda. The Dutchmen were pushed only twice, once by Beaver Creek and once by Hills, but, after a four-point victory in their second game against Hills, they won their final five regular-season games by an average of thirty points, highlighted by their back-to-back victories over Slayton and Luverne, two of the district's large schools.

Ellsworth, upset the previous year by Edgerton in the District 8 semifinals, finished the regular season 15 and 3, two of the losses being to Edgerton and the other to Magnolia. The Panthers only had back from the previous season's team 5-foot-11 guard Lee Visker, but first-year coach Mert Johnson, a former Augsburg College athlete, was receiving steady overall play from a lineup that included seniors Visker and 6-foot-4 Ron Hansen, and juniors 6-foot-3 Junior Boelman, 6-foot-2 Gary Colwell and 6-foot-1 Duke Lenderts.

Pipestone, however, was difficult to bet against. Although considered to share pre-tournament co-favorite honors with Edgerton, the Arrows possibly were given the edge based on strength of schedule and the overall play of 6-foot-4 senior Sid Bostic. The Arrows, ranked statewide throughout most of the season, were 14 and 4 playing against schools at least two and three times bigger than the majority of Tri-County Conference schools. Their four losses were by a combined eleven points: 53 to 51 against Canby, 58 to 54 against Jackson, 61 to 58 against Marshall, and 59 to 57 against Walnut Grove in overtime.

Pipestone lost three of its first six games but won eleven of its last twelve and was led by Bostic, who finished the season averaging 27.7 points, a statistic bolstered by his forty-five points against Marshall and forty-three points against Worthington. He broke nearly every Pipestone High and Southwest Conference scoring record in his senior year and was named, along with Veenhof, to WCCO radio's annual all-state basketball team.

Six nights after their exhilarating victory over Luverne, the Dutchmen returned to the court, prepared to begin tournament competition, sports' version of double jeopardy. The undefeated record may have helped bolster the confidence of the Dutchmen and their supporters—even help make all forget the previous season's loss to Jasper—but a couple of thoughts had to be troubling. Certainly, the loss of Roos made depth questionable, and Veenhof's history of foul problems couldn't be ignored.

History certainly didn't favor Edgerton. In the thirty-four District 8 tournaments, only seven schools claimed a title: Luverne winning seventeen championships, Pipestone seven, Worthington five, Slayton three, Jasper two, and Fulda and Lakefield one each. Jasper and Lakefield were the only two small-school teams to reach the Region I tournament.

Unbeaten regular-season records were not uncommon among the state's small schools, but it also was not unusual to see them eliminated in the districts where the larger schools prevailed. In the last five seasons, more than twenty schools from towns of all sizes entered tournament time undefeated, but only eleven advanced to the regional round. In 1959, Atwater, Forest Lake, Wood Lake, and Hawley finished the previous regular season unbeaten, but only Hawley, population 1,270, claimed a district championship; Wood Lake, population 506, had back-to-back perfect regular seasons but was eliminated each time in the District 9 tournament.

Edgerton had reason to be mildly concerned that Magnolia or Hills could scuttle its bid for the school's first district title. Magnolia had the rugged Voss and was coming off an 82 to 57 victory over Round Lake, a romp in which Voss and Jerry Ackerman had bookend twenty-seven-point efforts. The Bulldogs lost twice to Edgerton in Tri-County Conference games, but having lost the second by only twelve points, Ackerman said his team had hope.

"We had a pretty decent team with one weakness," Ackerman said, "and unfortunately Edgerton capitalized on that weakness."

The Bulldogs effectively patrolled Veenhof early in the game and loomed within eight points after eight minutes, but Verdoes hit four consecutive baskets early in the second quarter, and the Dutchmen were on their way to a 79 to 53 victory and a second-round Friday showdown against Hills, who defeated Chandler. Edgerton's five starters finished in double figures, led by Verdoes' twenty-one points and Kreun's seventeen, while Voss had a game-high twenty-four for the Bulldogs.

Less than twenty-four hours later, Edgerton was poised to meet Hills before a standing-room-only crowd in the Luverne gymnasium. Hills held the Dutchmen to fourteen points, and Edgerton led by only six points after eight minutes, but that small advantage prevented the Blue Jays from controlling the ball and the game's tempo. The Dutchmen broke loose in the second period on their way to a 72 to 41 triumph. Olson's bench accounted for the entire fourth-quarter scoring, but Veenhof still gathered twenty-six points and Verdoes sixteen before they left the game.

Later, Hills' coach Goehle would tell Corky Brace, the *Worthington Globe* sportswriter, that he thought a major reason for Edgerton's incredible season was its unselfish play.

Basketball pandemonium had been permeating Edgerton and the surrounding area since the Dutchmen's jack rabbit start. The public school's tiny gymnasium was packed for every game, with fans arriving an hour or more before the tip-off, hoping to secure a seat or even standing room in the tiny quarters. So, when Pipestone defeated Luverne, 77 to 54, to forge the Edgerton-Pipestone semifinal, the partisan response was seismic.

Although the two schools were only fifteen miles apart and had a basketball history stretching back to the 1930s, they hadn't played since 1955-1956 season after which Pipestone severed its regular-season ties with the Dutchmen. Since defeating the Arrows 46 to 44 in double-overtime in 1952, the Dutchmen had lost eight consecutive games to the Arrows, four coming in district contests. What Pipestone sportswriter Len Hart described as one of the district tournament's all-time semifinal pairings became a sellout the moment tickets went on sale.

Edgerton fans were waxing enthusiastic about their team's chances, and their praise of Olson crescendoed with each victory, but Pipestone fans equally were confident in their Arrows and proud of what Coach Ed Otto had accomplished in his third season. Granted, Otto began the season with the bellwether Bostic and Bruce Johnson, a pair of excellent college prospects, but he also had to rebuild his lineup after losing expected starters during the summer. The Glasrud brothers, senior Bob and sophomore Dave, had moved to Rochester and were starting for John Marshall High, while 6-foot-3 Ron Archer had moved to California.

Bob Glasrud was a 6-foot-4 forward who complemented Bostic—not unlike Edgerton's Verdoes to Veenhof—and Dave Glasrud was a 6-foot-1 guard who handled the ball well and played tenacious defense. Bob went on to become the Big Nine's second leading scorer, finishing the season with an 18.7-point average, just a fraction behind Austin's Gary Schumacher. Otto added that Archer was an outstanding prospect whom he believed might have wound up being the best of the three.

"It almost killed me when I learned the Glasruds were moving, and then Ron Archer, who might have been the best of the three, came to my house and said, 'Mr. Otto, we're moving to California,'" the former Pipestone coach said. "I almost cried. If we had had those three guys, [Edgerton] would have had a tough time matching up because we would have been big. However, Bostic just kept improving. Johnson was a fine player. And a kid named Doug Hart, a 6-foot-3 sophomore, really stepped up. Despite losing the other three guys, that was probably still the best team I had while I was at Pipestone."

As if the neighborhood rivalry and the game's importance weren't enough, fans eagerly anticipated seeing formi-

Bob Glasrud missed a chance to help Pipestone win District 8 title, but played a role in the 1963 South Dakota State NCAA championship.

dable centers Veenhof and Bostic together on the court. The weather forecast warned of a snowstorm, and the road conditions already were hazardous, but the game attracted a crowd that exceeded the capacity of the Luverne gymnasium. The game met the expectations of most, with the 66 to 52 final score belying an intensely competitive contest in which Edgerton didn't pull away until the fourth quarter.

Pipestone jumped to a 9 to 0 lead in less than four minutes, but Olson called a quick timeout and from that point the Dutchmen settled down. They trailed by five after one period, rallied to lead by one at the half and took a six-point lead into the final eight minutes when they gradually took charge despite having played the entire game without a substitution. The Dutchmen deftly handled Pipestone's pressure defense thanks in large part to the vacation-break scrimmage against Tracy, and although Bostic scored twenty-six points, the Arrows' center never took charge as he had done so many times in his career—although it was Verdoes and not Veenhof who defensively held Pipestone's ace in check.

"When I scouted Pipestone, I noticed that Bostic scored more off his rebounds than he did with his first shots," Olson said. "So, I put 'Duce' [Verdoes] on Bostic. I told him to stay in Bostic's face and keep him off the offensive boards. Bostic scored, but most of his points came after the fact."

Early, Olson's strategy appeared slightly misguided. Verdoes quickly picked up two fouls, and Pipestone held a nine-point lead, but after Olson called his timeout, the Dutchmen steadily worked their way into contention. Verdoes didn't pick up another foul, although he only scored six points, Kreun finished with fourteen and Wiarda added twelve.

Darrell Kreun drives for the basket against Pipestone in Edgerton's District 8 semifinal victory over the Arrows. The Dutchmen went on to win the district title.

"Bostic was stronger than me, faster than me, better than me," Verdoes said. "He was a great player with great quickness, and he could play both inside and outside. But we had great players, too. Veenhof was unstoppable, and I got a lot of help on Bostic. There is no way I could have handled him alone."

In his thirteen basketball seasons at Pipestone, Otto had fonder moments, such as when his Arrows defeated eventual state champion Marshall, but from time to time he looked back to that semifinal game against Edgerton. Otto profoundly respected Olson and his team and all they accomplished that season, but he couldn't help but wonder what might have been had the Arrows won the game.

Arrows fans—many convinced that their team was bound for Williams Arena and the state tournament—harshly criticized Otto and frequently reminded him of the loss every year when the state tourney rolled around. The feisty coach adopted a patented response, "Yes, they beat us, but they beat everyone else that season, too."

As for Bostic, the Edgerton game became an indelible memory from his high school days. He conceded that he and the team not only expected to defeat Edgerton but also win the region and play for the state championship. "Our expectations were to win the district, the region, and play in the state tournament," he said. "We had a substantial lead early in the Edgerton game and never should have lost that game, but that's easy for me to say because I was on the other side.

"And Edgerton had a wonderful team; after all, they went on to win the state tournament."

Denied the goal of most every high school player, Bostic ultimately lived an even greater dream. He was recruited by South Dakota State University and had a hall-of-fame career that was highlighted by a 1963 National Collegiate Athletic Association college division championship in Evansville, Indiana. Bostic made a forty-foot mid-court basket at the buzzer in a 44

Pipestone star Sid Bostic couldn't get the Arrows a state tourney bid, but scored the winning basket in the 1963 South Dakota State NCAA championship.

to 42 victory over Wittenberg of Ohio, seconds after Bob Glasrud—who transferred to SDSU from the University of Minnesota—hit a conventional field goal to tie the game.

"Sid was an extremely competitive player who accomplished a great deal with his strength," former SDSU teammate Nick Brod said. "Glasrud was so smooth and had an exceptional court sense. They not only played a major role in the championship game, but were an integral part of our entire success that season."

Glasrud was a role player, but Bostic was an impact competitor on a team that included 6-foot-10 center Tom Black, who would play with several National Basketball Association and guard Wayne Rasmussen, a three-sport SDSU standout who became a starting defensive back for the National Football League's Detroit Lions. In an era when the NCAA denied college freshmen varsity eligibility, Bostic scored 1,079 points and gathered 804 rebounds over three seasons. The Jackrabbits failed to repeat in Bostic's senior season, but he was named the 1964 North Central Conference's most valuable player, having averaged 17.4 points and 12.3 rebounds.

While Bostic was left to deal with college recruiters, the Flying Dutchmen braced for the championship game against Worthington. The Trojans finished the regular season 8 and 8 and defeated a 17 and 3 Ellsworth team to forge the first Edgerton-Worthington basketball matchup since the 1949 District 8 final when the Trojans prevailed 36 to 32. By now, Edgerton's believers were legion, but after defeating one of the state's highest-ranked teams, the Dutchmen themselves were cautiously optimistic.

"After winning what was the biggest game in which we'd ever played, we were confident we could handle Worthington . . . but not overconfident," Kreun said.

Edgerton celebrates its victory over Pipestone in District 8, the first time since 1952 the Flying Dutchmen had defeated their neighborhood rival.

Worthington, the district's largest school, matched Edgerton shot-for-shot in the first several minutes. The Trojans led by two points midway through the first period and shared a tie at the six-minute mark, but the multifarious Dutchmen found their stride and streaked to an 84 to 65 victory on a memorable Saturday night when more than 2,600 fans packed the Luverne gymnasium.

The Trojans controlled Veenhof in the first half, limiting him to twelve points, but while they concentrated on the Edgerton center, Kreun hit eight long-range field goals to lead the Dutchmen to a ten-point half-time lead. Worthington hawked Kreun more closely in the second half, but that simply allowed Veenhof and Verdoes to have their way inside. The Dutchmen took an eighteen-point lead entering the last quarter, allowing Olson to use his entire roster before Jasper's Henry Tschetter, District 8 committee chairman, presented the championship trophy. Veenhof scored thirty-four points, three more than Trojans guard Gene Puhl's career-high total. Kreun gathered twenty-two points and Verdoes added sixteen.

The Flying Dutchmen beat Worthington for its program's first District 8 title, but seemed more reserved than the night they beat Pipestone.

Edgerton left Luverne with its first district basketball championship trophy and a twenty-two-game winning streak, but the Dutchmen had little time to celebrate. In less than seventy-two hours, they would travel to St. Peter where Edgerton would be one of four teams vying for the Region II title in St. Peter's George B. Myrum Memorial Field House, home court to Gustavus Adolphus College basketball.

When the state tournament regional series began, Edgerton was one of only three unbeaten teams remaining in Minnesota, the others being Dodge Center in Region I and Forest Lake in Region VII. Duluth Morgan Park eliminated previously undefeated Duluth Central, Cloquet, and Esko en route to the District 26 title. Danube, led by sophomore Bob Bruggers, eliminated previously unbeaten Renville in District XII.

Once again, Edgerton's perfect record was a major source of pride but did nothing to enhance its position in the Region II bracket. Teams simply weren't seeded, and the Dutchmen were paired against two-time defending champion Mankato in the first round, while Mountain Lake and Sherburn met in the other game. The winners would play two nights later for the Region II berth in the state tournament scheduled for March 23 through 25 in Minneapolis.

In a pre-tournament column, *Worthington Globe*'s Brace cited some of the obstacles confronting Edgerton in the Mankato game, foremost the Scarlets' distinct size advantage as well as recent tournament experience and familiarity to the Myrum Field House court, an elevated surface approximately fifteen feet longer and fifteen feet wider than Edgerton's home court—68½ feet by 34 feet—and the home courts of Edgerton's Tri-County foes.

He wasn't, however, counting out Edgerton, emphasizing that the Dutchmen had an excellent chance to win if they continued to shoot the ball as well as they had from the season's outset through district play.

Mankato, the largest school in the region, was indeed a menacing draw for the Dutchmen. The Scarlets, who in their tournament debut lost to eventual champion Wayzata 57 to 51, returned this time without all-tourney selection

EDGERTON

Jim McArthur and other starters, but rebuilding wasn't that difficult at one of Minnesota's largest out-state schools. The Scarlets finished tied for second in the demanding Big Nine Conference and, entering the Region II opener, had an 18 and 4 record. Among their wins was a 62 to 53 victory over Big Nine champion Austin and two of their four losses were decided in overtime.

History also was on Mankato's side. The school had been represented fifteen times in the state tournament since the district-region format was adopted, while District 8 hadn't produced a Region II champion since Luverne triumphed in 1938. In the previous ten tournaments, District 8 won only two first-round games—Luverne winning both, but also losing a 1957 first-round decision to tiny Pemberton, population 147. In regional play a year earlier Jasper—the team that defeated Edgerton for the district title—was eliminated immediately by Westbrook, 57 to 48, with the latter losing to Mankato by eight points in the final.

Regional tournaments generally represented midnight for most small-town Cinderella teams, the classic example being Kennedy, a tiny hamlet tucked in the extreme northwest corner of the state. From 1955 through 1957, Kennedy zipped through three consecutive regular-seasons and District 32 tournaments undefeated, but each time lost in Region VIII, twice to Bemidji and once to Thief River Falls. Kennedy's three-year record was 79 and 3, but they never reached Williams Arena.

"I can remember driving over to St. Peter for a practice before the region, and I had part of the team in my car," former Edgerton school superintendent Bill Fure said. "I don't remember who it was, but one of the kids said, 'All the teams are going to be tough . . . but then we're pretty good, too.' They had that attitude. They didn't feel the pressure to win because they won the district, something no other Edgerton team had done."

In its preparation for the region, Edgerton had one major gauge by which to judge Mankato's strength, that being the film of the Mankato-Austin game. Olson found the film, provided by former Dutchmen coach Bill Standly, now an assistant at Albert Lea, to be extremely valuable in establishing his matchups against the burly Mankato line-up. Recognizing Mankato's strength on the boards, his major emphasis was screening out on every shot.

"I remembered Bill Monat always saying, 'He who controls the boards controls the game,'" he said referring to his junior college coach. "If we didn't block out, we weren't going to get many balls with the exception of possibly a few from Veenhof and Verdoes. We couldn't afford to give them second shots."

The Scarlets knew little about Edgerton, but they shared their local newspaper's opinion. As they rolled over Pemberton, Amboy, St. James, and Mapleton in the District 6 Tournament, they were keeping an eye on the west, knowing that District 6 would play the District 8 champions in the Region II opener. What they saw was this unknown tiny town of Edgerton defeating the teams they deemed most likely to represent District 8, particularly highly regarded Pipestone and Worthington.

Few pundits or even loyal Flying Dutchmen fans gave Edgerton a chance to win. Mankato coach Orville Schankl, sensing his team shared that sentiment, warned the Scarlets not to be overconfident. Mankato starter Leroy Schweim possibly best summed up his team's pre-tournament mindset.

"I can remember the date and the time and everything about it," the former guard said. "We're on the bus;

it's two below zero on a Tuesday afternoon, and we're headed to good ol' Myrum Field House for a 3:00 p.m. game against Edgerton. In that field house, the court was elevated, and it seemed like we could fly.

"We thought we were going to win; that was it. I remember thinking, 'This is going to be fun,' . . . but it wasn't."

Thousands witness Edgerton's surprise rout over mighty Mankato.

Mankato's fun lasted through the warm-ups in which the band of wide bodies sprinted out in their sleek uniforms and repeatedly dunked the ball with resolve. The Dutchmen, a bunch of skinny kids wearing faded, ill-fitting uniforms, droopy sweat socks and worn Converse shoes, went about their business but couldn't help but be distracted by their opponents' panache. Edgerton forward Bob Wiarda remembers being "scared as hell" and even the stoic Stevens said to no one in particular, "How are we going to beat those guys?"

If Mankato's flamboyant pre-game routine was an exhibition, then the ensuing thirty-two minutes could be described as an Edgerton clinic, one which confirmed to many Mankato partisans among the 2,500 fans in attendance that the Dutchmen's twenty-three-game winning streak was no fluke. Veenhof put Edgerton ahead thirty seconds into the game and finished with twenty-four points in a 73 to 44 victory over the dazed Scarlets. The Dutchmen hit fifty-three percent from the floor against a team whose success was tethered to a resilient defense. They made thirty-one of forty-three free-throw attempts, and held their own on the boards in a beginning-to-end romp.

Wiarda recalled standing along the lane late in the third quarter. Kreun was at the free-throw line, and Edgerton held a commanding lead when he noticed the Mankato player next to him staring. "He was looking at me up and down, gazed up at the scoreboard, and then turned to me and gave me the once over again and said, 'Where in the hell did you guys come from?'"

Veenhof was one of four Dutchmen in double figures. Kreun, shut out in the first quarter, finished with seventeen while Verdoes and Graphenteen each had eleven points— Verdoes seven-for-seven from the free-throw line. George Riley led Mankato with sixteen points and Schweim had fourteen, while Veenhof held Clark Westphal, Mankato's 6-foot-5 center, scoreless and kept him off the boards.

"I absolutely never played against another team like that," Schweim said. "It was like they all were almost in everyone else's mind. People still talk about them, but unless you saw it you can't comprehend the depth of it. I can look people in the eye and say, 'I lived it.'"

And lest one thinks Schweim's account is strictly hyperbole, listen to his wife, Bette, who laughingly defined the impact the contest had on her husband's memory of his basketball past.

"He can forget my birthday. He can forget our anniversary. He can forget all the mundane things in life," she said, "but he remembers every play of that game."

In the second game of the Tuesday double-header, Mountain Lake, a team that defeated Jackson in overtime to win the District 7 title, needed two overtimes to eliminate Sherburn, 69 to 68. In a frenetic contest in which neither team owned more than a five-point lead, regulation ended in a 67 to 67 deadlock, with Sherburn's Dennis Gettler missing the front end of a one-and-one free-throw situation with no time remaining. The two teams traded turnovers in a scoreless first overtime, but in the sudden-death second extra period—the first team to score two points declared the winner—Mountain Lake's Dick Grantz, unable to get the ball inside to ace Charles Dick, nailed a twenty-foot jump shot seconds after Sherburn's John Krohn failed to gain the winning two-point margin when he missed one of two free-throw attempts.

Mountain Lake coach Mack Nettleton had little time to ponder the victory. The first thing he did was call his

Dean Verdoes scores against Mankato in the Region II semifinal game.

pregnant wife, Janet, two days overdue, and then devise a game plan to prepare his Lakers, 18 and 4, for the Thursday night Region II title game against the sharp-shooting Dutchmen who several hours earlier had embarrassed Mankato.

"Edgerton made a believer out of me when they moved through a tough district by defeating Pipestone and Worthington," the former University of Minnesota player told *Minneapolis Tribune* columnist Sid Hartman. "And if there were any doubts, those were removed when they walloped a big, strong Mankato team.

"You watch them standing on the floor and they don't look like much. Once they start playing, they operate like they have been playing in the barnyard since they were able to hold a ball. Watch out for Edgerton. If they beat us, they could go all the way in the state."

Olson and his team remained to watch the Mountain Lake-Sherburn game before returning to Edgerton, and

Dean Veenhof scores two of his twenty-four points en route to the Region II title.

Olson left the Myrum Field House optimistic about his team's chances, knowing his Dutchmen matched up much better against Mountain Lake than they had against Mankato, the team they had manhandled that afternoon. Not that he shared his sentiments with his players.

"It would have been disappointing if we hadn't beaten Mountain Lake after the way we played against Mankato," Olson said. "But we just went about our business and did what we had to do to get ready for the game. I told my players that every team at that stage was dangerous . . . and Mountain Lake certainly. They had a good team and I had a great deal of respect for their coach."

Outsiders were most likely wont to give Edgerton the edge in the Region II championship game. Not only had the Dutchmen defeated two of the state's top teams, Pipestone and Mankato, they defeated Luverne by eleven points not long after the Cardinals defeated Mountain Lake, 66 to 48, during the regular season. Mankato players such as Schweim expected the Dutchmen to win easily.

But Mountain Lake was a town steeped in basketball tradition going back to the tournament's formative years. The school was runner-up in the first state tournament held in 1913, and the Lakers had made thirteen state tournament trips, returning home with the 1939 title. And although

Mountain Lake is no match for Edgerton's Verdoes (left) and Veenhof.

Nettleton was a first-year high-school coach, he had guided the 1958-1959 Gopher freshman team after completing his varsity-playing career. The Lakers just had defeated a 16-and-3 Sherburn team, so Nettleton, his players, and residents from a community with a population of 1,943 were conceding nothing.

The Lakers quickly jumped to a four-point lead, but Edgerton calmly found its stride, and midway through the first quarter pulled ahead to stay in what would be a 61 to 55 victory. The Dutchmen led by eleven points after three periods, but Mountain Lake wouldn't go away and Edgerton was forced into a ball-control game to thwart the Lakers late rally. Veenhof, who avoided foul problems for the sixth time in as many tournament games, scored twenty-four points to pace the new regional champs, followed by Kreun with sixteen and Wiarda with twelve. Mountain Lake and Edgerton each had twenty-two field goals, but the Dutchmen shaped the winning margin by outscoring

Edgerton fans packed Myrum Field House for the Region II final, but reached home in time to greet their triumphant Flying Dutchmen.

EDGERTON

Mountain Lake seventeen to eleven from the free-throw line.

Nettleton's son, Curt, was born less than twenty-four hours after the game, but years later the coach's memory of the Edgerton loss remained vivid. Without pausing, he discussed the contest as if delivering a post-game interview.

"In the first half, Kreun hit six of eight field long-range shots, and we were playing good defense. He was a threat once he crossed the ten-second line," Nettleton said. "In the second half, we stopped him, but they simply started dumping the ball inside to Veenhof. We ran a zone press that ate up lot of teams during the season, but not Edgerton. They had no problem, and a few times Verdoes dribbled right through it."

At the conclusion of their improbable march through the region, the Edgerton players gleefully celebrated the moment, hollering and triumphantly waving their arms as they lifted Olson on their shoulders. In the stands, former Dutchmen coaches Ken Kielty and Bill Standly celebrated with hundreds of Edgerton fans, delighted that the town had finally realized its longtime dream. Meanwhile, the Lakers were left to dwell on what might have been, particularly the team's mainstay Charlie Dick.

"It was always my dream for us to be state champions because my uncles were on Mountain Lake's 1939 state championship team," Dick said referring to Henry and Ruben Epp. "I wanted to do what they did. I guess I fell a little short, but it was a great run, and losing to the eventual state champions made it easier to take."

Once the ecstatic Edgerton fans completed their revelry in St. Peter, the celebration moved to Edgerton, with the team greeted outside of town and escorted to the tiny school gymnasium where it was honored in an early Friday morning ceremony. Afterward, the resilient Dutchmen fans sang happy birthday to Marlys Olson, who hours earlier had received the gift of a lifetime.

Proud Dutchmen surround Coach Rich Olson, who holds the championship trophy after defeating Mountain Lake.

CHAPTER SEVEN
The Legend Evolves

Edgerton's atmosphere crackled with excitement over the next several months, save for Sunday morning worship in all of the town's five churches and day-long family prayer. On the Friday after the regional victory, cards and letters came pouring in from former Edgerton High students and faculty, rival towns, and even strangers who waxed delight in the small town's triumph. Fure even received a note from his former college coach, his former athletes from his Chatfield coaching days, and a special congratulatory letter from the former Lynd basketball coach who led his tiny school's basketball team to the 1946 state final before losing to Austin.

Lost in the excitement of Edgerton's milestone season was the incredible performance of the Christian School's 118 to 54 victory led by junior Bruce Timmer, son of an Edgerton minister. The 6-foot guard scored fifty-two points on twenty-two field goals and eight free throws and collected twenty-six rebounds. The Eagles started the season with four consecutive losses, but finished 12 and 6 led by Timmer's 18.5-point average. Timmer's family left for Hanford in central California after his sophomore year, and he started two seasons for a large public school team in California.

Timmer and his younger brother, Doug, were major losses—Doug having become a high-school All-America in 1964 while at Hanford—but the Southwest Christian still had 6-foot-4 Norm Prins to lead the Eagles basketball team in the next couple seasons.

"Edgerton was a good place to grow up in, and there was a lot of basketball talent scattered around there," Timmer said. "I can remember wondering, 'Would have I been good enough to play for that team?'"

Along with victory came more celebrity than anyone could have imagined, or in the words of Bill Pool, implement dealer and Edgerton's Civic Club leader, "Those boys have really put our town on the map." The *Enterprise* and *Worthington Globe* enhanced their Dutchmen coverage, but reporters and photographers arrived from nearby Sioux Falls and several larger Minnesota newspapers including the *Minneapolis Star-Tribune*. They chronicled the everyday life of the state's most recent basketball "Cinderfellas," their coaches and parents and Main Street businessmen. In addition to myriad newspaper interviews, photographers asked the players to pose in a variety of venues: sitting in class, sipping milkshakes at Jolink's Pharmacy, and playing pinball in the other local teen haunts.

Even the shy Kreun volunteered to jump up and click his heels for a photo on Main Street and Veenhof, another bashful Dutchman player, posed for pictures on the Veenhof farm, spending time with his family and his teammates.

Bob Wiarda shares a victory malt with girlfriend Toni Moss.

Dean "PeeWee" Veenhof is assisted by brother Merle in barnyard play.

In almost every photo, the small-town players were wearing weird black hats, vintage Buster Keaton, atypical for teens in the era or that area. "Rich told us at the beginning that we had to wear hats and overshoes because he didn't

Forced by Olson to wear hats, the Dutchmen select "stylish" chapeaus.

want any of us getting sick," Verdoes explained. "So, we figured that if we had to wear hats we'd wear the silliest hats we could find." That represented the closest thing anyone could interpret as teen rebellion among the Dutchmen.

School continued through the week, but most players, band members, cheerleaders, and other students conceded that concentration on school work was difficult because of the excitement and the media blitz on the town. Superintendent Bill Fure did an outstanding job maintaining at least some semblance of order for the students and faculty.

The two busiest men in town were Fure and Olson. While Olson prepared his team for the tournament, Fure—in addition to his administrative and teaching duties—arranged the team and band transportation, coordinated the tournament-week logistics, and coped with an unwieldy ticket situation. In a complicated system, Edgerton received 310 first-round reserve and general-admission tickets, 206 for adults and 104 for students. The allotment was based on school enrollment, and Fure's first concern was meeting the needs on a priority list that included student and family members, Edgerton faculty, and the season's drivers who had taken the farm kids home after practices. Fure furiously attempted to secure more to meet the demand, but it was painfully obvious that all needs would not be met.

The ticket situation became even stickier as the Dutchmen advanced, and Fure, working out of Room 215 in the Curtis Hotel, spent much of his time as a ticket manager, sending any extras he could obtain to Jolink's Pharmacy for sale. Some of the most avid Dutchmen fans made the 195-mile drive to Minneapolis daily to secure a ticket, and many of the fortunate ones still had to drive back home that night because they lacked Twin Cities housing or had to do chores.

Edgerton basketball boosters J.H. Brovold (left), Cliff Peterson, and Fred Baldwin flash what was the toughest ticket in Minnesota.

Olson, named WCCO Radio's "Coach of the Week" for his team's performances in district and region play, participated some in the media blitz but spent most of his time running practice and fashioning a plan. His preparation included a 500-mile weekend round-trip drive to Duluth. Rich and Marlys Olson left for Duluth early Saturday morning so Rich could scout the Region VII championship game, knowing that Edgerton would play the winner in the state tourney's opening round. They stayed at his family home in Virginia that night and returned to Edgerton the following day.

"We got to Duluth near game time. The game was sold out, and I didn't have a ticket," Olson said. "I talked to the tournament chairman, and he couldn't help but finally got one from Marsh Nelson, a friend who was a television guy in Duluth. He could only get me one ticket, so my wife had to drive our car to Virginia, sixty miles away, and I came back after the game with my brother Ralph and his buddies from Gilbert.

Chisholm defeated Duluth Morgan Park 60 to 51, earning the Bluestreaks their school's first tournament berth since1940, and Olson returned with a six-page scouting report written on both sides. It wasn't until he returned that he heard of the Saturday afternoon car accident involving Veenhof, Kreun, and their mothers when they were returning from a shopping trip in Luverne.

On a slick tar road east of Hardwick, Veenhof was driving the family's 1954 Dodge and Kreun was sitting in the front seat with him, while ahead of them was area farmer H.J. Hanamann on a tractor pulling a pair of wagons loaded with baled hay. Hanamann took a left and, while the tractor and first wagon cleared Veenhof's path, the car collided with the second rig, severely damaging the right-front side of the passenger side of the Dodge. Kreun intuitively scrambled toward Veenhof, and everyone avoided injury, saving Hanamann from becoming Pipestone County's number-one public enemy.

Next to the state tournament, an accident was the week's major story.

"Everything happened so fast that it

didn't seem that bad," Kreun said. "The car was damaged pretty badly, but that was it. Nothing happened. Not a bruise. We were fortunate because it could have been a lot worse."

Once Olson was assured that no one was injured, he heaved a sigh of relief knowing first that Edgerton had been spared a tragedy, and second that on Thursday they would make a well-deserved appearance in the state's premier sports event. Little did he know the Dutchmen would provide the state with an indelible memory that would last into the twenty-first century and beyond.

On Tuesday afternoon, minutes before the Edgerton basketball team departed for Minneapolis, an estimated 2,000 well-wishers attended a Main Street pep rally for the players and coaches, Rich Olson and his assistant John Rath. Olson thanked the community for its support, expressed his pride in the team, and alluded to the rural image in which his players were being portrayed by the state's media.

"I know that people like to talk about our small-town boys, and they think we won't be able to find our way around the big city . . . or that we might get lost in Snyder's Drug Store," he said with a Cheshire smile. "But we know our way around on the basketball floor. They're all good [state tournament teams] when you get this far, but we have a good team, too."

Odds were definitely stacked significantly against Edgerton, the eight-team field's smallest town. In fact, not only was Edgerton the smallest town, the community had two high schools and Edgerton Public had a smaller enrollment than Christian School just down the street. Add to this Edgerton's imposing tournament draw. If the Dutchmen defeated Chisholm, which had an enrollment

Edgerton holds a pep rally on the Flying Dutchmen's tiny home court.

five times larger than Edgerton's, they would meet the winner of Richfield and North St. Paul, the second and third largest schools in the tournament.

Edgerton fans give the Dutchmen an enthusiastic send-off to the Twin Cities.

EDGERTON

If community support meant anything, the Dutchmen were off to a fantastic start in what was possibly the most exciting event since the inaugural Dutch Festival in the early fifties. Speakers included Olson, community and school leaders, and the Christian School's student president, extending best wishes from his school's peers and administrators.

The Edgerton and Pipestone bands provided the music, the cheerleaders led the rally songs, and when the ceremony ended the 24-and-0 Dutchmen were piled into a three-car caravan that was given a police escort out of town. The Edgerton band, directed by Harlen Wesselink, left a couple days later on a bus that took them to the University of Minnesota campus where, between Williams Arena performances, the nearly forty members were housed in university dormitories for three days. What equipment and luggage that couldn't be transported on the bus, Jim Roelofs transported to the U of M campus in the decorated "Flying Dutchmen" pickup.

If there was a moment when the team may have been at least temporarily distracted from basketball, it was near the end of a 200-mile journey when the Minneapolis skyline, highlighted by the Foshay Tower, pierced the clouds. Until this, Worthington or Pipestone represented big-city life, and Sioux Falls, South Dakota was their Gotham.

Or if the skyline wasn't a temporary distraction from their goals, perhaps pulling up to the enormous Curtis hotel, tournament headquarters for all eight teams and their travel parties, was. Posh hotel living was a luxury to which most were unaccustomed. Once settled into the Curtis hotel, the Dutchmen spent the remainder of Tuesday sequestered in their rooms, save for a team meal

Edgerton's favorite sons catch a glimpse of Minneapolis before the busy tournament week.

in the dining area and a trip to Hennepin Avenue where the *Worthington Globe* took a picture of Edgerton's top six players basking in Minneapolis' neon-lighted main street.

"That week we were isolated, locked away from the world," Verdoes said. "We played hearts, penny poker, and watched television. Everything we did, we did as a group and security was tight."

On Wednesday afternoon, clad in the white shirts and tie they were required to wear, outside of their rooms, the Dutchmen attended a luncheon at the Leamington hotel where all the tournament teams were honored. From there it was back to the Curtis until late afternoon when the team made the trip down Washington Avenue to Williams Arena for a forty-five minute shoot around that began at six o'clock. The facility, the nation's largest indoor campus arena at the time, was in stark contrast to their tiny Edgerton dimly-lit gymnasium. The springy Williams Arena court was ninety-four feet by fifty feet, more than a third larger than the firm Edgerton court. The backboards were glass instead of wood, and if anyone had done the math he would have figured that the 19,000 seating capacity would hold the combined population of the Tri-County Conference towns, with Pipestone and Luverne tossed in.

"It took some time to get used to the venue. I'd never seen a place like that in my life," Kreun said. "It was huge, and it had all those seats. I remember someone saying, 'Boy, you could get a lot of bales of hay in here.' It was really a highlight, but by the time we began the game against Chisholm that Thursday, we were hardly aware anyone was there."

The fans, however, would definitely arrive in record numbers, beginning Thursday and running through Saturday night, but, before taking a seat, they were well versed on all eight teams thanks to the Twin Cities media hype. From the time the players arrived, reporters and radio and television sportscasters interviewed the players, coaches, or anyone else involved with what was March Madness, long before the term was coined. And, as was the custom, the smallest schools attracted much of the early attention, meaning the Dutchmen received more than their fair share of public attention.

By game time, it was common knowledge that Edgerton was the only undefeated team in the field. The town's population was listed as 961, but, by the 1960 Census that hadn't been released, the community now had 1,019 residents. Edgerton High's enrollment was ninety-four, about a third of Granite Falls, the next smallest school in the field. They were aware that not only was Edgerton making its first state tournament appearance, the school was the first since Luverne in 1938 to represent District Eight in the state's premier high school event.

Individually, 6-foot-5 Dean Veenhof was no complete stranger, having been named to the WCCO all-state team earlier in the tournament series, but the remaining Dutchmen were relatively anonymous before their opening game. Dean Verdoes received some attention for his lofty scholastic standing, and Tom Warren, a 5-foot-5 reserve guard, was singled out as being the tournament's shortest player.

Two years earlier, Edgerton's coach was a high-scoring Macalester star, but his celebrity this week involved his youth. At twenty-three years of age, he was the tournament's youngest and least experienced coach. The media relished emphasizing his youthful appearance and how he preferred milk but drank coffee so people could distinguish him from his players. Ove Berven even quipped that Olson looked younger than some of his Austin players, and the lead item in one newspaper's notes column revealed that Olson was not even born when Berven began his career at Spring Valley, Wisconsin, in 1933.

Acquiring the sentimental role was easy for any small-town team. Sustaining it beyond the opening round was difficult. Carlton, population 860, was runner-up a year earlier to Wayzata, a Twin Cities suburb, and Lynd, population 292, was second to Austin in 1946, but in the post-World War II era the two schools were the exception to the rule. Olson was a basketball junkie well versed in the state's perennial balance of power and the tourney history; no one had to advise him on the imposing task confronting the team.

"When I looked at our draw for the state, I said, 'Holy cow, when are we going to get a break?' For starters, I knew how tough Region VII can be because I grew up in that area," Olson said, referring to his opening game against Chisholm. "Then came Region V, which is the toughest in the state . . . at least according to them, and then there was Austin and Ove Berven, who had won more state tournaments than anyone.

"But we were just happy to be there, and we were just going to play our game, that's all."

In Chisholm, Edgerton would face a 22-and-1 team that had won fourteen consecutive games since a loss to Greenway of Coleraine shortly after the Christmas break. The Bluestreaks were a physical force led by 6-foot-3½ Bob Dropp and 6-foot-5 Jasper Brancich, and they had guards that could handle the ball and shoot it. Chisholm appeared similar to Mankato in size and girth, but, based on Olson's

Chisholm, Edgerton's first-round opponent, was 22 and 1. Members were: (front row) Ron Novoselac, Brad Skarich, Bob Dropp, Jasper Brancich, Ken Kekke, Tom Radotich, and Ed Klotzbach; (back row) Coach O.J. Belluzzo, John Huska, Dave Hannan, Gerald Bogda, and Don Stahl.

scouting report, the Bluestreaks shot the ball better than the Scarlets. Dropp was the team's leading scorer with a twenty-point average, and he combined with Brancich to give Chisholm exceptional rebounding strength.

The Bluestreaks were coached by O.J. "Ner" Belluzzo, a member of Chisholm tournament teams from 1932 through 1934, and he was in his sixth season since replacing his high-school coach Harvey Roels. The Blue Streaks were appearing in the school's first state tourney since 1940, and Belluzzo, whose 1934 team won the state title, made no attempt to disguise his delight. "After having been in the tournament three times as a player, it's a realization of my dreams to return as a coach," Belluzzo said. "I'm getting a thrill a minute."

Richfield, Edgerton's second-round opponent, was 22 and 2. Members: (front) Dennis Johnson, Mac Lutz, Roger Alevizos, Bill Davis, Bill Szepanski, Bob Sadek, and Harry McLenighan; (back) Gary Bystedt, Doug Barton, Bob Werness, Mark Gjerde, and George Lary.

EDGERTON

Times, however, had changed since he was a player. The 1934 Bluestreaks scored fifty-seven points in three state tournament games, but in this season had scored fifty-seven or more points in fifteen contests.

In the bracket's other half, North St. Paul was 22 and 4 and Richfield was 22 and 2. The two Twin Cities suburban powers didn't play during the regular season but scrimmaged during the Christmas break.

North St. Paul relied heavily on Coach Hal Norgard's trademark "Buzz Saw Defense," a full-court pressure scheme that he applied throughout, and the offense was led by 6-foot-2 Don Arlich and 6-foot-1 Larry Hansen, two all-tournament selections from the Polars' 1959 fourth-place team that lost to eventual runnerup Carlton, 50 to 49 in the semifinals. In the Region IV final, North St. Paul defeated St. Paul City League co-champion Mechanic Arts, coached by former NBA Lakers and major league baseball starter Howie Schultz.

Richfield lost only to Lake Conference foes Bloomington and St. Louis Park in the regular season and breezed through district competition. A week earlier, the Spartans completed a romp through Region V, defeating Minneapolis West by nineteen points and perennial District Twenty power Willmar by twenty seven points. Bill Davis, a 6-foot-6 center high on many college recruiting lists in basketball and baseball, was the centerpiece of an extremely athletic group. Six roster players played for the 1959 Minnesota Legion baseball championship team, and when starters Davis, Bob Sadek, Dennis Johnson, Bob Werness, and Mac Lutz went to the University of Minnesota, each played at least one varsity sport.

Austin appeared to have the upper hand in the upper half of the tournament bracket. The Packers (16 and 4) opened against Thief River Falls (17-6) and Granite Falls (16 and 7) was matched against Melrose (23 and 1). Granite Falls and Austin were members of the 1959 Minnesota Elite Eight, Thief River Falls was making its first appearance since 1939 and Melrose was a first-time qualifier.

Granite Falls returned with three starters and a couple key reserves from the 1959 tournament, and although longtime coach Leonard Espeland had retired, the Kilowatts were guided by the capable Dick Nielson, who, after leading tiny Carlton to second-place a year earlier in the state, was lured to western Minnesota to be a teacher-coach at Granite High and play town team baseball for the Kilowatts. Granite Falls got off to a poor start, losing five of their first seven games, but for good reason. Standout Gerald Hegna, an all-state tournament player in 1959, missed much of the season after breaking his leg in a football game against Ortonville, and Keith Anderson was hampered by a knee injury. Once Granite got healthy, the Kilowatts took charge, losing only two of its remaining regular-season games and won District Eleven and Region III for the school's fourth state tournament berth since 1947. Granite had only modest size, but played a steady up-tempo game led by the sturdy Hegna, Anderson, and Lyle Hemingson.

Melrose, the "other" Dutchmen team in the field (although not the Flying variety), lost its only regular-season game to eventual Catholic League state runner-up St. Cloud Cathedral, and capped an eleven-game winning streak with region victories over Detroit Lakes and Crosby-Ironton. The Dutchmen had no starter taller than 6-foot-1, so they relied on a fast-break offense, balanced scoring, and a pressure defense that produced a series of come-from-behind victories.

EDGERTON

Thief River Falls was coached by Hartley Story, who three years earlier guided Walnut Grove out of Region III into the state tournament. The Prowlers survived the rugged Region VIII tournament with a lineup anchored by 6-foot-7 center Ron Hanson, 6-foot forward Bob Pearson, and 5-foot-9 guard Steve Embury, the team's floor leader. They were beaten twice by Bemidji in the regular season, once by twenty-six points and the second in overtime, but after defeating once-beaten Argyle in their region opener, Thief River Falls upset Bemidji, 60 to 53, to end the Lumberjack's seven-year reign in the region.

Thief River Falls enjoyed a spectacular winter, with both the basketball and hockey teams qualifying for state tournament play, a double that was last achieved by Roseau in 1946.

Finally, Austin, third in 1959 and champion in 1958, returned for the third consecutive season and for the fourteenth time in Berven's twenty-one-year career as the Packers' coach. He had only one returning starter with which to build, but that player was Clayton Reed, who like Davis was a highly-recruited athlete in two sports. Several reserves stepped up from the season before, but no one better than 6-foot guard Gary Schumacher, the Big Nine scoring leader with an 18.7-point average. The 6-foot-5 Don Bulger, whose father played on Berven's first Austin team, also improved enough to fortify a front court that helped the Packers survive previously undefeated Dodge Center 54 to 53 in the Region I final. Reed, also an all-state football end, was a third-year starter who played in every minute of Austin's 1958 championship season.

Richfield was the consensus favorite among the eight tournament teams; in fact, the venerable Butsie Maetzold, former Hopkins coach whose Warriors won the 1952 and

Austin, Edgerton's final opponent, was 18 and 4. Members: (front) Manager Lance Jacobson, Clayton Reed, Don Bulger, Paul Campbell, and Manager Jack Schmeider; (middle) Earl Butler, Bill Krueger, Bill Booher, and Dick Golberg; and (back) Lyle Kline, Terry Brown, Gary Schumacher, Mitchell Page, and Charles Draheim.

1953 state championships back to back, predicted that the Spartans would win. Richfield not only had the biggest, fastest, and arguably the strongest team in the field, the Spartans qualified for the tournament on the Williams Arena court and represented Region V, which won six of the eight previous state titles.

Austin lost to Richfield early in the season by fifteen points, but Austin was given serious consideration based on the Packers' tradition and Berven's reputation. This was the twenty-second state tournament for the Big Nine team, which since 1939 failed to reach the Williams Arena basketball festival only five times. While many expected Austin and Richfield to meet in the championship game, Berven certainly counted out no one in the field, considering his team's narrow Region I victory over Dodge Center. "The small schools aren't afraid of us anymore," he said after the region final.

Reflecting on the eve of the opening round, Olson said that he was concerned by the team's lack of depth. When Jim Roos broke his arm near the end of the season, Daryl Stevens became the lone experienced reserve, an unsettling thought when one considered Veenhof's frequent foul problems. Beyond Stevens, who was three inches shorter than Roos, Olson's roster consisted of "B" squad graduates with only token varsity time and who by any measure were ill-prepared for tournament play. Still, the brash young coach maintained more than a scintilla of hope that his team could win it all. They were, after all, the only undefeated team in the field and had proved their mettle in victories over highly-touted Pipestone in the district and Mankato in the region.

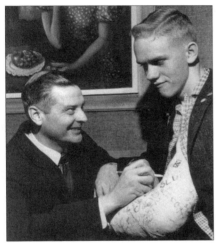

Radio announcer Dick Enroth signs the cast of the injured Jim Roos.

"We were small and skinny. We weren't the best-dressed team in the tournament by any stretch of the imagination," Olson said. "I don't want to say that our uniforms were raggy, but they were pretty close.

"I thought we had a good chance to win because [the players] had done everything I'd asked of them. They were unselfish, they didn't care who scored, and they took care of the ball. When they committed a turnover, you had to think a while to remember the last time they had given up the ball."

If Rich Olson believed in his Edgerton team, his brother Ralph was confident enough to make a wager on the Dutchmen and let it ride for the tournament's duration. Olson didn't remember how much his brother bet, saying only that it was a significant sum for the era, and Ralph, considering the money and brotherly love, earned every cent of the profits in the Richfield game alone.

CHAPTER EIGHT
The State Tournament

On Thursday, March 24, the Minneapolis Lakers met the St. Louis Hawks in the Minneapolis Armory, scene of Game Six in the NBA West Division playoffs. The Lakers, led by the incomparable Elgin Baylor, had a 3 to 2 lead in the series and a chance to close out the Hawks at home, but the contest attracted only 7,956 fans.

The Lakers were Minnesota's lone major professional franchise at the time, but they weren't about to upstage the Minnesota State High School Tournament's opening day in Williams Arena where 17,413 spectators attended the afternoon session and a record 18,436 gathered for the evening double-header.

While the Dutchmen remained sequestered in the Curtis hotel, waiting for their evening game against Chisholm, Granite Falls defeated Melrose 44 to 42, and Austin eliminated Thief River Falls 55 to 41 in the second game.

The Granite Falls and Melrose game got the tournament off to an exciting start in a game that went down to the last shot. Melrose held a three-point halftime lead, but couldn't shake the Kilowatts who rallied to tie the game through three quarters. Melrose countered and held a six-point lead with less than four minutes remaining, but at that point Granite Falls applied an effective full-court press. The strategy forced a series of Dutchmen turnovers, and the Kilowatts launched an eight-point run, completed by Lyle Hemingson's pair of free throws that gave the Kilowatts a 44 to 42 lead with a minute and a half remaining. Melrose had a final chance to force overtime, but Marvin Ostendorf's long jumper caromed off the rim shortly before the buzzer. Hegna and Hemingson paced the winners with thirteen points each.

Austin struggled early with Thief River Falls and the Prowlers' 6-foot-7 center Ron Hanson, but the Packers held them to two third-quarter points to forge a twenty-point lead and coasted in. Clayton Reed turned in a spectacular performance, scoring twenty points and collecting twenty-one rebounds, while Hansen paced the Prowlers with seventeen points. Austin was now 6 and 1 in the last three state tournaments.

Around the time Granite Falls was completing its victory, Edgerton players were finishing their pre-game meal and, after gathering their gear, were wedged into three taxis and escorted to Williams Arena. In the locker room, the Dutchmen were quiet, but according to Olson the mood seemed no different than before playing Pipestone, Mankato, or Mountain Lake.

"Kreun never seemed excited about anything," Olson said. "Either did Verdoes, and anyone who has ever doubted that he is our team leader is wrong. Veenhof was

The Dutchmen brace for their tournament opener against Chisholm.

our go-to guy, but Verdoes was analytical . . . did things right and that had a calming effect on our team. That was a major intangible with this group."

Once on the floor, the players—almost to a man—insisted that they block out the crowd and experienced no anxiety in the pre-game warm-ups while many in the record crowd of 18,436 were wondering how this scrawny bunch of Dutchmen with a pair of 5-foot-8 guards reached the tournament, and how the team would stand up against the burly Bluestreaks. But unlike the Mankato game—perhaps because of it—Edgerton concentrated on their pre-game routine and paid no attention to the players at the other end of the court.

There may have been smirks, even some cynical chuckles when the Dutchmen came out for warm-ups, but, if there was any question they belonged in the tournament, they answered the skeptics with a 65-to-54 victory, a mild upset and a major achievement considering that the 6-foot-5 Veenhof sat out fifteen minutes because of foul trouble. The lanky center was dynamic underneath early, scoring eighteen points and collecting ten rebounds to help build Edgerton's eight-point lead, but he picked up his fourth personal with five and one-half minutes left in the half and was pulled.

"[Veenhof] was definitely our go-to guy," Verdoes said, "but we could play without him. We just kept laboring away and whatever happened, happened."

When Veenhof left the game, Verdoes, Kreun, and Wiarda continued to do their thing and Stevens did a yeoman's job in relief. The Bluestreaks pulled within three points twice after Veenhof went out, but the Dutchmen increased their lead to ten by the intermission, 34 to 24, and were up by thirteen points when Veenhof returned to start the fourth quarter. He finished with twenty-four points and Kreun added seventeen, but Verdoes' overall contributions arguably made the major difference. He scored fifteen points, grabbed eight rebounds, and picked up only one foul while holding Chisholm's Dropp to thirteen points, seven below the Bluestreak star's season average.

Dean Veenhof battles Chisholm's Jasper Brancich on the boards.

"Going into the game, we were concerned about Dropp, and again I turned to Verdoes, and he did a great job," Olson said. "When Veenhof went out, there was no way that I was going to take Verdoes off Dropp, so I put Wiarda, who was barely 6-foot-2, on Brancich. Then it was simply a matter of how long we could play without Veenhof."

Edgerton hit nearly fifty percent of its field goal attempts and outscored Chisholm 27 to 12 from the free throw line, taking advantage of twenty-nine Bluestreak fouls. Chisholm coach O.J. "Ner" Belluzo rated the Dutchmen as "one of the best shooting clubs I've ever seen, this year or any year." Ron Novoselac, a starting Chisholm guard, also expressed for the Dutchmen's prowess, but was puzzled by Chisholm's heavy foul load.

"The fouls were really crucial," he said, adding that the team averaged only fifteen personal fouls a game. "I was the only starter who didn't foul out, and I had four . . . and I don't remember having four fouls in a game all year."

In the day's final game, Richfield and Bill Davis flexed their muscle in a showdown between Minneapolis and St. Paul suburban league teams. Davis scored twenty points despite missing time with stomach cramps to lead the Spartans to a 60 to 51 decision over

Chisholm's Ron Novoselac drives the lane on LeRoy Graphenteen.

the North St. Paul Polars. Coach Hal Norgard thought his team's trademark pressure defense did a reasonable job on Davis, who had a batch of thirty-point games in the regular season and tournament time, but was at a loss to explain North St. Paul's thirty-two percent shooting. "We had good open shots, but we simply weren't hitting," Norgard said. "Our defense was good and so was our rebounding, but it wasn't our night to hit. I felt we needed sixty points to win, and we'd have topped that if we shot like we did in the Region IV tournament."

The result was a semifinal game between Edgerton and Richfield, a David and Goliath match-up. Goliath remained the consensus favorite and destined to meet Austin in Saturday's championship game, but David had become a huggable sentimental favorite by most everyone outside of Richfield's city limits.

The Dutchmen saw only the first couple minutes of Richfield's game before Olson had them transported back to the hotel, but any player who read a Friday morning paper knew that they faced an imposing task in Friday evening's semifinal game. Richfield hadn't been tested throughout the tournament season and had the state's most highly-recruited athlete in Davis, not only an outstanding center but an ace pitcher for a Richfield American Legion team that won the 1959 Minnesota state title.

But any apprehension on the Dutchmen's part was concealed by their stoic disposition and their unyielding trust in Olson. "Rich always had us well prepared," Verdoes said. "He'd tell us who we were going to guard and how to guard them. He could watch [the opposing team] a few minutes and spot things right away. He was extremely observant . . . very clever."

Or in the words of Veenhof, when asked in the regional tournament how Edgerton planned to play Mountain Lake: "I don't know, but I'm sure Ole will tell us how to play . . . he'll think of something."

After watching Richfield defeat North St. Paul, Olson left with a profound respect for the Spartans, impressed by their overall size, strength, and athletic talent. Richfield's reputation definitely didn't exceed its ability, but Olson still maintained faith that his team was capable of finessing its way past another top-notch opponent, just as the Dutchmen had done against Pipestone and Mankato.

Back home in Edgerton, tournament fever reached epidemic proportions after the Dutchmen defeated Chisholm. Many of the town's residents attended Thursday night's game, but suddenly those who listened to the game on the radio or traveled to area towns to gain better television reception wanted to be in Williams Arena on Friday night. Bill Fure had a new allotment of Friday-night tickets— one hundred for adults, fifty for students, and "token tickets" for seventy-seven adults and fifty-two students. The token tickets were dispensed in the probability that some of the schools whose teams lost in the opening round would return at least a portion of their allotment. Even with that, Fure—camped in Room 215 in the Curtis Hotel—knew he was going to need more and was working the phone like a Las Vegas bookie to acquire them. Residents with no tickets or token tickets made the nearly two-hundred-mile drive to Williams Arena in hope of securing a seat for the semifinals; some of them were farmers who returned immediately after the game to do chores with little or no sleep. Some Edgerton fans abandoned hope of getting a ticket but made plans for a drive to Windom,

Marshall, Redwood Falls, and even Montevideo—one hundred miles from home —where they hoped to find an establishment with a television and good reception.

In Minneapolis, the Dutchmen players spent another afternoon watching television, playing cards, or napping while a sparse crowd watched the consolation session in which Melrose defeated Thief River Falls and Chisholm defeated North St. Paul. It would be a long day for the Dutchmen, who weren't scheduled to take the court until approximately 9:00 p.m., following the Austin and Granite Falls semifinal opener.

A record crowd of 18,812 turned out for the evening's semifinals game, and the fans were treated to an excellent opener between Austin and Granite Falls. The Packers bolted to an early seven-point lead and defeated the Kilowatts 67 to 58, but between Austin's early lead and the final score, Granite bounced back every time the Packers were poised to tuck the game away. Granite Falls trailed by thirteen points with nearly six minutes left in the third quarter, but rallied to tie the score, 44 to 44, and trailed by only two points with 3:49 left. But the Packers made a resolute six-point run to take charge, and for the second time in three years the Packers were in the championship game.

The opening game's action, however, paled in contrast to the Friday nightcap. Former players and older fans still deem the game to be one of the most exciting, or in some cases THE most exciting, as any they've ever seen or with which they've been associated. From the moment the teams reached the court, those in Williams Arena and those watching the telecast or listening to the broadcast were held hostage by the epic clash between country and city kids. Perhaps Davis, the heralded Richfield center, provides the most vivid description of the prevailing fan sentiment.

Cheerleaders (left) Mona Gilman, Judy Zwart, Mavis Kreun, and Margie Griffin do their job on the Williams Arena sideline.

"I was captain of the team and led us out of the locker room and up the stairs into the arena," he said. "My first impression was the size of the crowd . . . the place was packed. The second was that, for the first and only time in my athletic career, we got booed . . . right out of the chute. Once the game began, it took on a life of its own."

Back in Edgerton, Harry Verdoes, Dean's father, listened to the WCCO broadcast of the game. The Spot Café's owner attended Thursday's game with his wife, Frances, older son, Gene, and daughter Carol, but returned home that night and the next day went back to work. Business wasn't that brisk in a half-deserted town, but some patrons hung around and listened to the broadcast with the nervous father.

Duane Kreun, one of Darrell's brothers, was working in Sioux Falls and had used all his personal time to attend the region tournament, so he couldn't get out of work for Thursday's game and didn't get off on time to make the trip Friday evening. "After work we took off and kept stopping at bars until we found good reception," Duane said of the Chisholm game. "The next day someone told us about a place much closer and so we went there from work.

"I went to Minneapolis on Saturday and saw the game in Williams Arena. I can't remember how I got the ticket, but I got one."

About tip-off time for the Austin and Granite Falls game, John Bolt and Arlo Den Ouden were exchanging wedding vows in Edgerton's First Christian Reformed Church. The wedding reception was well underway when the Edgerton and Richfield game began, but the Dutchmen weren't ignored. The master of ceremony provided regular updates to the new couple and their guests and even the pastor, G.S. Kok, admitted that he was pleased that the ceremony had been concluded before Edgerton played.

"I guess it was around Christmas time when we scheduled the wedding," Bolt explained. "[The Dutchmen] were having a good season, but at the time we never really thought about them getting into the state. We had planned to honeymoon in Denver after the wedding, but we cancelled that, and I bought tickets at the drugstore for Saturday, figuring we'd at least get to see them in a consolation game.

"We were lucky. A friend of mine got us reservations at a hotel somewhere downtown, so we had our honeymoon in Minneapolis."

In Friday morning's sports sections throughout Minnesota, the Edgerton and Richfield game was the lead

EDGERTON

story—even with the Lakers and St. Louis poised for Saturday night's seventh and deciding game in the NBA West—with special attention focused on the showdown between Davis and Veenhof, the former relying on physical force and the latter finesse. One newspaper feature, topped by a headline reading, "Davis Eager to Duel Veenhof," the latter said he had watched some of the Edgerton and Chisholm game and was impressed by the Dutchmen center. "I'm sure he'll be the finest center I'll face all season," he told reporters. "I've always wondered what I'd do against a boy like Veenhof. Now, I'm going to find out."

At the outset, Davis and the Spartans appeared to have a distinct edge, jumping to leads of 8 to 1 and 10 to 3, but then Veenhof and Kreun went to work and Edgerton tied the game before guard Bob Sadek's long jumper notched Richfield's 14 to 12 first-quarter advantage. The teams were tied five times before Edgerton claimed its first lead with less than five minutes remaining and the Dutchmen held on for a 30 to 28 advantage at halftime.

Richfield bounced back early in the third quarter, 36 to 34, on Doug Barton's outside basket, but Veenhof—having his way underneath—led an eight-point Edgerton run that

Richfield's Bill Davis (#43) and Bill Szepanski challenge Dean Veenhof.

A dejected Dean Veenhof watches the Richfield game after fouling out.

underscored Edgerton's 44 to 41 lead after three quarters. Edgerton increased its lead to six early in the fourth quarter, but with five minutes and nine seconds remaining and the Dutchmen leading 52 to 46, Veenhof fouled out.

The 5-foot-11 Stevens came in as a forward and the 140-pound Verdoes was moved inside to guard the burly Davis, a mismatch that imposed two tolls: Davis scored freely enough to forge a 54 to 54 tie and Verdoes began to pick up fouls in his attempt to contain Davis. Edgerton regained the lead when Graphenteen sank a pair of free throws, but Davis came right back to forge another tie at 56—his tenth point in a twelve-point Richfield burst.

Edgerton came up empty in its next possession, and Richfield, claiming the ball with eighty seconds remaining, elected to hold the ball and give the towering Davis the last shot. The plan was solid, but the execution was flawed when a three-second lane violation was called on Richfield's Mac Lutz with eighteen seconds remaining. Years later, Richfield's Sadek—Lutz' long-time friend—didn't challenge the official's integrity but did question his discretion under the circumstances.

"Mac, who was setting a screen for Bill, had a 13- or 14-size shoe and his foot may have been on the line, so technically he was in the lane," Sadek said. "You'd see guys camping out in the middle many times and it wasn't called, so why would it be called in that situation?"

Veenhof, an observer with five fouls at the time, has shared Sadek's sentiment. "I've even wondered for nearly fifty years if he committed the [lane] violation, and second, whether it should have been called," he said.

Dean Veenhof (left) and Darrell Kreun close the lane on Richfield's Bill Davis, while Bob Wiarda (far left) and Dean Verdoes lend backup to support Coach Rich Olson's sagging man-to-man defense.

The game, however, was far from over. Edgerton missed a desperation basket, and a three-minute overtime ensued. Minus Veenhof, the smaller Dutchmen were at a significant disadvantage, and fourteen seconds into the overtime, Verdoes fouled out for the first time in his career. "I wouldn't have fouled out if I hadn't wound up guarding Davis," Verdoes said, smiling, years later. "I never worried about fouls because I could play without fouling. But Davis wasn't just big, he was talented."

Davis now became the ward of Wiarda, a muscular farm kid with a big heart, but still only 6-foot-1 and twenty to thirty pounds lighter than the Richfield ace. Wiarda, the two other starters and Stevens were joined by Larry Schoolmeester, a 6-foot-1 sophomore "B" squad member who had no quality varsity time but was called up to fill the tournament roster.

"I'm sitting at the end of the bench where I always sat and suddenly I hear the guys down the line saying, 'Schooly, Schooly, Schooly, Schooly,' and I realize Ole is calling for me," Schoolmeester said. "I went into the tournament figuring that the only way I'm ever going to get to play is if we're way ahead or way behind, but this happened so fast that I didn't have time to get nervous. I just went in there not wanting to make any mistakes and do my job defensively."

Schoolmeester remembers touching the ball only a couple times as Edgerton went into a holding pattern, with Graphenteen and Kreun doing the majority of ball-handling. The objective was to find a seam in the Richfield defense or draw a foul. The Richfield defense hung back at first, but eventually moved out to challenge the guards and with less than two minutes left, Kreun was fouled and converted both ends of a one-and-one situation. With Edgerton leading 58 to 56, Davis got the ball inside with sixty-eight seconds to go, but, squeezed by Wiarda and Stevens, the center traveled. At that point, Wiarda made one of the few

Dutchmen mistakes of the night, fumbling a pass from Kreun on a fast break. Sadek was fouled seconds later, but missed the front end of a one-on-one, much to the relief of many, but to Wiarda in particular.

"I really thought that I had lost the game," Wiarda said, explaining his feelings as Sadek stepped to the line. "I began passing the ball before I even caught it. I wanted to find a hole to crawl in."

The many moods and emotions of Edgerton Coach Rich Olson.

Graphenteen was fouled immediately after Sadek's errant free throw attempt and the guard, chomping wildly on his gum, sank two free throws to put Edgerton up by four points. Sadek made amends for his missed free throw, hitting a jump shot that cut the Dutchmen margin back to two, but Davis was forced to quickly foul Kreun. The personal was Davis's fifth, so he was eliminated, and Kreun converted two free throws into a 62 to 58 Edgerton lead with only fourteen seconds in the wild contest.

Sadek was fouled four seconds later and made two free throws to bring Richfield within two points again, but once again Richfield was forced to foul, and, with six seconds on the clock, Graphenteen stepped to the line for the second time in overtime. The junior guard sank the first free throw, making it a two-possession game, and turned his attention toward the bench, winking and flashing an elfin smile while placing his thumb and index finger together to flash the okay sign. "I don't remember seeing it," Olson said of the playful gesture. "I was pretty much tied up at the time."

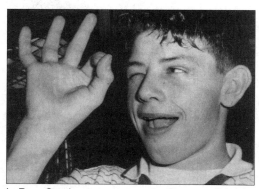

LeRoy Graphenteen re-enacts the everything-is-okay sign he gave Olson.

Graphenteen sank the second, but the meaningless free throw was negated when he went over the line, and when the clock read 0:00 the Dutchmen advanced to the state championship game, scheduled to begin Saturday night at 9:30. They shot a tepid thirty-six percent from the field, had ten less field goals than Richfield, and had two starters on the bench down the stretch, but thirty-five free throws in forty-three attempts—seventeen in the final eleven minutes—sent Edgerton into the championship game against Austin.

Coach, players, and cheerleaders sprinted onto the court. The fans who weren't from Richfield loudly expressed their delight. And the media had begun pounding out a story for the ages . . . all in the media with the exception of Corky Brace, the *Worthington Globe*'s veteran sports editor. He was just re-entering the arena after skipping the overtime.

"Friday night during the overtime period with Richfield, the pressure was too great," he explained in his daily column "BRACE'S BITS." "If Edgerton was going to lose, this writer didn't want to be there to see it. We should have had more faith in Dick Olson's reserves and the poise of the Dutchmen that has been demonstrated too often."

In Edgerton, Harry Verdoes's heart was still doing flip-flops, telling a reporter that knowing his son had fouled out gave him "the heebie-jeebies. The Bolts and their wedding party were celebrating the second most important event of their night, but the bride's grandfather, Nys Den Ouden, confessed to a Twin Cities reporter that the wedding "would have been a flop if Edgerton would have lost." And in some town, in a bar whose name Duane Kreun couldn't remember years later, the brother who inspired Darrell Kreun's interest in basketball, rejoiced not only for Darrell and his teammates but for the program in which both he and his other brother, Ron, had played earlier in the fifties. "I'm not a real emotional kind of guy," Duane said reminiscing, "but I remember jumping on a table when they kept fouling Darrell and LeRoy. The most nervous I've ever been was when they played Richfield."

Back in Williams Arena, it was a tale of two locker rooms, with the atmosphere in Dutchmen quarters mixed between jubilation and relief, more of the latter than the former. The proverbial ice that ran through the veins of Graphenteen and Kreun during the game had apparently melted, with the diminutive guards conceding to being nervous down the stretch. Kreun scored four free throws in the overtime, highlighting his team-high twenty-one points, and Graphenteen scored the other three and finished with fifteen points. "I wouldn't want to go through that again," Graphenteen said. "In fact, I'd rather not have to shoot those free throws again, either."

The two most relieved players in the arena were Veenhof and Verdoes, deeply relieved to know that

Edgerton's championship run hadn't ended while they sat helplessly on the bench.

"It was painful when Veenhof fouled out, and it was more painful for me when I got my fifth foul because, with both of us out, you sense the chances weren't very good," Verdoes said. "We were very, very fortunate to have won. They were a very good team. They were bigger than us. They were faster than us. They were stronger than us. But we managed to make enough free throws in the last quarter and overtime."

Gene Farrell lamented his team's missed opportunities, particularly with both Veenhof and Verdoes on the bench, but at no time did he demean Edgerton. In fact, after consoling his players, the Richfield coach walked to the Dutchmen locker room to congratulate the team for its gritty effort and wish them good luck. "You played a wonderful game," he said. "Get a good night's sleep tonight and go all the way tomorrow. You deserve it."

In the Richfield locker room, Davis said he "cried like a baby, just like everyone else." When the tears dried, the Spartans demonstrated their class, making no excuses and commending Edgerton's play. "Next year, Dean Veenhof will be the finest center in the state . . . nobody will come close to him," Davis said. "They didn't even take any time at the foul line. They just walked up there and fired away," Denny Johnson said. And to the media, the Richfield coach commended the Dutchmen and their coach: "You know, Olson has done a great job with that team," he said, "and [the team's] poise is simply unbelievable."

Bob Sadek, a 6-foot-2 Richfield guard, said that the year after the loss, he and a group of teammates seriously considered trying to line up a rematch, even if it meant driving 200 miles to Edgerton. The Spartans harbored no ill

EDGERTON

will against the Dutchmen, only a competitive fire to atone, but their whim never came to fruition.

"We enjoyed playing them, and the game created some memories for us and certainly them," Sadek said decades later. "But it still hurts. We would have loved to win."

Later in the sixties, when Sadek was doing his student teaching, he chose Virginia in northern Minnesota where Olson coached and taught after leaving Edgerton. The game was relived a few times, but Sadek also discovered where the Dutchmen acquired some of their fire during some noontime one-on-one sessions with the fiery Olson.

On the morning of the state championship game, while the Dutchmen rested and Olson pondered strategy, Fure continued to receive ticket requests. He began answering the phone at 7:30 a.m. and continued to do so until leaving for Williams Arena. His Saturday allotment included one hundred adult and fifty student tickets, plus ticket tokens for seventy-seven adults and fifty-two students. Ticket tokens were sold on a first-come basis, with the number available contingent on how many tickets participating schools returned to the Minnesota State High School League. The MSHL provided seventy-seven more tickets, and Austin—which received a much larger allotment based on enrollment—turned over one hundred and ten adult tickets and another fifty for students.

Radio stations were even assisting the superintendent, asking those with tickets they didn't plan to use to help Edgerton out, and some listeners responded. But supply still appreciably exceeded demand, and some disappointed Edgerton fans resigned themselves to catching the game on radio or finding a city restaurant or bar with good

TV reception. In Windom, an estimated one hundred and fifty men and women reportedly assembled in Eddy Schneider's Brass Side to watch the game on television.

The Lakers were in St. Louis for the deciding game in their seven-game NBA series, but even if the game had been played in the Twin Cities, the toughest ticket in town would have been the one to get you into Williams Arena. The game attracted a tournament-record 19,018 spectators, running the weekly count to a record 85,846 spectators. Imagine the amusement of Pat [Kooiman] Wassink, who, while cleaning out her parents' home many years later, discovered an unused ticket for Saturday night's championship game.

Before Saturday night's contest, Edgerton's image was enhanced when Richfield drubbed Granite Falls 77 to 50 in the third-place game. Davis was emotionally drained less than twenty-four hours earlier, but he bounced back to score forty points and finish the tournament with a near-record eighty-six in three games. "After the Edgerton game, I felt bad . . . down in the dumps," Davis said. "But we had another chance to play, so we just went ahead and played it."

Chisholm defeated North St. Paul on Friday but lost to Melrose 65 to 57 in the consolation final.

An Edgerton and Austin final was immediately compared to the 1946 championship game between Austin and another tiny school in Lynd. The Packers defeated Lynd, less than an hour away from Edgerton, 66 to 31, but although Austin also might have appeared to have an edge on the Dutchmen, it would have been absurd to predict another Packers blowout. The Dutchmen were 26 and 0, including victories over Mankato and Richfield, two teams that defeated Austin in the regular season.

EDGERTON

Berven might have had more than twenty-five years experience over Olson, but the former Macalester star demonstrated a coaching acumen far beyond his years. He had assembled a disciplined and patient team that shot the ball well, played with uncanny precision, made few mistakes and played sound defense.

In John Kundla's daily commentary in Saturday's *Minneapolis Star-Tribune*, the University of Minnesota basketball coach implied that the Dutchmen might be emotionally drained after their overtime victory on Friday night, but that was one of Olson least concerns. "They never got extremely high after a win," he said, "and after a loss . . . well, they hadn't lost."

By Saturday evening, Edgerton's fan base was enormous, and when the Dutchmen took the floor they received a thunderous ovation that shook the Williams Arena foundation. Unfortunately, many "outsiders" who had adopted the country boys believed that to support them was to express disdain for their opponents, and the Packers were targets of countless boo-birds, far more boisterous than before the Richfield game. "The fans were really obnoxious. All of a sudden you realized there were 500 of them pulling for Austin and the rest hated them," Verdoes said. "Nobody wanted us to win," Don Bulger said speaking for Austin.

Preparing for the game, Berven and Olson were involved in a chess match of sorts. The Austin coach wanted to deny Veenhof the ball and decided to go with a zone, sagging off Graphenteen, who hadn't made a field goal in the tournament. Olson, anticipating Berven's strategy, told Graphenteen to shoot when given the opportunity, knowing that the guard's low scoring average belied his accurate touch.

"He averaged around six points a game, but the reason he didn't score a lot was because he didn't have to,"

LeRoy Graphenteen protects the ball from Austin's Terry Brown.

Olson explained. "Kreun was the shooting guard and LeRoy was what today they call the point guard. He did a lot of the ball handling, dished off to the open player and hung back to deal with the break when Kreun went inside."

Graphenteen, who took only two shots before the championship game, opened his assignment with an air ball, but if he flinched it was only briefly and not apparent. They were giving him so much room, he knew that he had to keep shooting, and he did. Austin's Clayton Reed hit the game's first basket, but Verdoes and Kreun put Edgerton into the lead, and Graphenteen, poised alone on the perimeter, hit back-to-back set shots. Once his marksmanship had been established, Veenhof chimed in. At the end of the quarter, Edgerton was leading 17 to 11, and the crowd was on their feet, deliriously responding to Graphenteen's closing shot of the period. Graphenteen had taken a pass at the

Edgerton end with only a couple seconds left and hurled the ball discus style into the basket seventy feet away. Nine years earlier, Gilbert's Andy Snyder made a similar shot en route to the Buccaneers' state championship, but Snyder's basket counted, and Graphenteen's was waved off.

"I definitely remember the roar," Graphenteen said. "I vaguely remember the official signaling that I had gotten the ball off too late."

Berven abandoned the zone for a man-to-man defense, a costly decision in that it played to Veenhof's strength. The Edgerton center took control underneath, scored the first four baskets of the second half, leading the Dutchmen to a 36 to 24 lead at intermission. The Packers went to a full-court press in the second half, but that played to Verdoes' strength. Pressure was designed to make a team hurry and make mistakes, but Verdoes wouldn't let that happen. He calmly guided Edgerton through the pressure, and the Flying Dutchmen continued their scorching offensive attack. They won the game 72 to 61 and a couple times led by as many as sixteen points.

Dean Verdoes and Austin's Clayton Reed fight for a rebound.

"The Austin game was almost relaxing compared to the Richfield game . . . sort of anticlimactic," Kreun said. "We didn't have anyone in foul trouble. We have very few turnovers, and we were able to control the ball."

Bob Wiarda challenges Austin's Gary Schumacher for a loose ball.

Veenhof scored twenty-seven points and grabbed fourteen rebounds and Graphenteen came next with fifteen, having hit five of eight field goal attempts and five of nine free throws. As a team, Edgerton hit 55.3 percent from the field. Clayton Reed, playing in his ninth consecutive and final state tournament game over three seasons, had twenty-one points and ten rebounds, but Edgerton's Wiarda held the Big Nine scoring leader, Schumacher, to ten points.

"Our shooting was not as good as it has been, but even at our best we would never have been able to match Edgerton's," Berven said referring to the Dutchmen's 55.3 percent accuracy. "You would have had to see it to believe it."

All season, Olson told them to play one game at a time, and suddenly there were no more games to play. The Dutchmen, representing the smaller of two schools in the smallest Minnesota town to produce a state champion, were 27 and 0, making the Dutchmen only the ninth undefeated champion in state tournament history. Depth was one of Olson's major concerns entering the tournament, and Edgerton's bench produced only three points in three games, but Veenhof, Verdoes, Kreun, Graphenteen, and Wiarda—a starting lineup for the ages—were solid throughout, and Stevens, the lone experienced reserve, was stellar in relief.

Since the Richfield game, Edgerton was referred to as a "team of destiny," but Berven flashed a rueful smile when the term was mentioned in a Sunday morning interview before the Packers left for home. "It's fine to be a team of destiny," he said, "but the thing that beat us Saturday night was a sound, tough basketball team with a great player in Dean Veenhof and the kind of shooting that demoralizes you."

Dick Seltz, Berven's assistant and a legendary high school baseball coach, found humor in the fact that some considered Edgerton's victory to be an upset. "Everybody wanted to talk about them coming from a small town," he said, "but we knew they were tough. They played a deliberate style. They could pass. They could shoot. They could do everything."

So solid and steady were the Dutchmen in three games, they received unprecedented recognition

Captain Dean Verdoes (left), Dean Veenhof, Darrell Kreun, and Coach Rich Olson holding the championship trophy after defeating Austin.

on the all-tournament team. Championship teams had generally been accorded three spots, but four Edgerton players were selected. Joining Austin's Clayton Reed and Gary Schumacher, Granite Falls's Harold Anderson, and Gerry Hegna, Richfield's Bill Davis and Bob Sadek, North St. Paul's Larry Hansen, and Melrose's Russ Sieben were Flying Dutchmen Dean Veenhof, Dean Verdoes, Darrell Kreun, and LeRoy Graphenteen.

The announcement left the four Dutchmen with a bittersweet feeling because Bob Wiarda had not been selected. Since they produced a perfect record playing a consummate team game, they assumed that the entire team should share all accolades.

"Sure, I was a little disappointed," Wiarda said of being the lone Dutchman out, "but the important thing was that we won the tournament."

Luck certainly played a role for a town with a population of 1,000 to produce a state champion, let alone a

Edgerton's Darrell Kreun, LeRoy Graphenteen, Dean Veenhof, and Dean Verdoes became first foursome selected to all-tournament team.

EDGERTON

small town with two high schools. Things might have been different if officials had let Chisholm play more aggressively or Mac Lutz hadn't been called for a lane violation late in the Richfield game or if Graphenteen hadn't delivered when Austin practically begged him to shoot.

Luck is almost always going to be a factor in tournament competition, but it would be folly to say that good fortune determined Edgerton's championship. Richfield's Bill Davis, extremely gracious in defeat, had so much belief in the 1960 Spartans that years later he suggested that in a five-game series between the two teams, Richfield possibly would have won three times. Certainly Pipestone, Mankato, Mountain Lake, and Chisholm also would have welcomed the opportunity to play Edgerton again, but players all know that it's one loss and out at tournament time.

Perhaps Edgerton's Dean Verdoes offered the most profound assessment of the Dutchmen's improbable journey . . . or for that matter any small town team that accomplishes the seemingly impossible.

"It was sort of a fluke but not a fluke because we were good enough to have won," he said. "When you start off with nearly five hundred teams and only one is standing at the end, that's a fluke . . . but that's the nature of sport."

CHAPTER NINE
The Celebration

E dgerton celebrated on the Sunday after its basketball team claimed the state's high school basketball championship, but not in the manner one might have expected in a community reveling in a major triumph.

Sunday was like any other Sunday in town. They celebrated the Sabbath, a day reserved for devotion, attending services in one of the five local churches, and spending time quietly with family and friends. Not even a hallmark occasion in the southwest Minnesota community was going to alter that commitment.

Out of respect for the day and to allow Edgerton residents time to prepare a proper welcome, the state's reigning champions remained in Minneapolis through Monday morning, with the Edgerton Civic Club paying for the extra day. But rather than sleeping in after three days of grueling competition, the players and coaches began Sunday the Edgerton way: They attended services at the Riverside

Community Reformed Church in Bloomington. Although more than two hundred miles from home, the services had a familiar feel. The pastor at Riverside was the Reverend William G. Wolbrink, who until 1957 spent eleven years at Edgerton's First Reformed Church in which seven Dutchmen players and team manager Doug Vander Beek were members.

The pastor's son, Dean, grew up with most of the Edgerton players. The Bloomington High junior visited the Dutchmen at the Curtis and attended every one of their games. He conceded he was mildly shocked when Edgerton defeated Richfield, a Bloomington Lake Conference rival, but he was not remotely surprised to see the Dutchmen in church less than twelve hours after winning the state title.

"I could not believe that they'd beat Richfield because I knew the difference in the Edgerton's school size and the size of Lake Conference schools," said Dean Wolbrink, who as a freshman had played basketball at Bloomington. "But no matter what would have happened in the tournament, my family and I would have been delighted to have them at our church. We welcomed them far more as old friends than as state champions.

"That they attended church that Sunday was understandable. That's the way it is in Edgerton, it's a go-to-church town. Many of the team members had grown up with me and my family, even before they started school. They were in church every Sunday for the eleven years we lived there, and they continued to attend services after we left."

The Reverend Wolbrink proudly introduced the Edgerton contingent and explained his association with the town and the players, but his sermon was about small towns in general and the existing bonds between the people and the Christian faith. He then turned to the Dutchmen.

EDGERTON

"Some people will ask why you don't go back home and have your celebration today," he said. "So, we'll explain to them that when God created the world, He established the seventh day as the day of rest, as the best day of the whole week. We try to keep this day different from the other days, to be respectful to the command of the Lord."

When the team filed out of the church, the players were greeted by an early-day version of the paparazzi, not unlike the days immediately before tournament week in Edgerton, and a flock of young autograph seekers who somehow learned that the Dutchmen were in the neighborhood. For the remainder of the day, whether they were dining at Cedric's restaurant, visiting John St. Marie at University Hospital, bowling at the Bloomington alleys where Olson had been employed a year earlier, or simply touring downtown Minneapolis, they experienced celebrity status.

"It was sort of gratifying and fun, but also weird . . . and we weren't particularly comfortable with it," Veenhof said of the celebrity. "We really didn't know how to handle the situation because we were just a bunch of small-town country boys who really hadn't begun to understand what had happened. In fact, we wouldn't realize what had happened until much later."

From church, the team was whisked to Cedric's Fine Foods in Edina for a steak dinner, courtesy of *Minneapolis Star-Tribune* columnist Sid Hartman. While at Cedric's, the team was introduced to Miss Emma Edgerton, ninety-five-year-old daughter of General Edgerton, for whom their town was named.

After lunch, Olson took his top six players to University Hospital to visit the fifteen-year-old John St. Marie, who contracted polio in 1952 and who less than a week

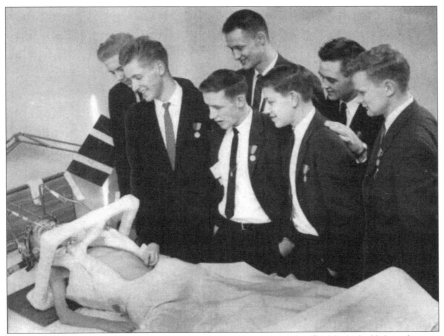

The Dutchmen's top six and their coach visit polio victim John St. Marie in University Hospital. St. Marie, was an avid Edgerton basketball fan.

earlier had undergone the second of three spinal fusion operations to straighten his back. St. Marie, an avid sports fan who since his childhood had enjoyed the Minnesota state basketball tournament, began to follow Edgerton in regional play and rooted for them through their three state tourney games. The visit was arranged by Stillwater sportscaster Jim McLaughlin, a friend of a former Olson teammate at Macalester.

"I didn't have an inkling that they were coming. A nurse told me that morning I was going to have some special guests in the afternoon," St. Marie said. "It was such a thrill to have watched them win the night before on television and then to see them in my hospital room the next day. The fact that a bunch of Dutch kids from a small town winning it all really appealed to me . . . they just wouldn't go away. Nothing intimidated them."

St. Marie's fascination with an underdog surviving major odds was understandable considering that, when he contracted polio at age eight, physicians told his parents he probably would live only two or three years because his severely curved spine hindered his breathing and was causing his vital organs to be cramped. But St. Marie said his love of sports sustained his resolve to live until science discovered a means to straighten his spine and eliminate the medical death sentence. The Minnesota state high school basketball tournament was his favorite event, so the Edgerton triumph and subsequent visit went far beyond the half hour he spent with the champions.

The team enjoys a leisurely Sunday afternoon sightseeing in Minneapolis.

"I've met a tremendous number of people who accomplished a great deal," said St. Marie, who graduated from St. Thomas College in three years and earned his law degree from the University of Minnesota. "But Edgerton's victory was probably the most inspiring sports event in my life, and you must remember that the 1960 Gophers went to the Rose Bowl."

The Dutchmen spent the remainder of the afternoon touring downtown Minneapolis and relaxing for the first time in several weeks. But although Minneapolis was a great place to visit, most of the players were eager to return home. "It was unbelievable, all the activities and the places they took us," LeRoy Graphenteen said. "I had never been to the Twin Cities per se, so when Darrell [Kreun] and I were walking around Minneapolis, I was seeing things and doing things I had never experienced. So, as far as I was concerned, it was sort of a nightmare."

Hours before the Dutchmen's 9:00 a.m. Monday departure from Minneapolis, hundreds of Edgerton residents had begun preparing the "Welcome Home" celebration for their state champions. Edgerton residents had given the Dutchmen a grand welcome after the Region II tournament and a royal send-off the day they left for the state, but both paled in contrast to the welcome they received in what several town officials described as the greatest day in Edgerton history. Some preliminary planning was conducted Sunday night, but the formal preparation began near dawn when Mayor John De Boer and William Pool, president of the Civic Club, met to organize the logistics and select a committee chairman. By noon, the community already was in near Dutch Festival or Fourth of July mode.

On Main Street, a large flatbed truck was parked in front of Jolink Pharmacy and converted into a presentation stage for the players. Elmer Kooiman drove to Sioux Falls to purchase banners and bunting to stretch across Main Street and to be draped from Main Street buildings. His wife, Thelma, directed the decorating. Edgerton School Superintendent Bill Fure had called ahead from Minneapolis on Sunday to cancel Monday classes so students were painting Main Street windows and signs. Someone scaled

169

the town water tower and painted, in large letters, "The Champs of 1960."

On a cold and overcast afternoon, the Edgerton High School band donned their summer Dutch marching attire, and Joyce Tinklenberg found three sets of Dutch costumes and wooden shoes for Mavis Kreun, Carol Verdoes, and Carla Veenhof—sisters of Dutchmen starters—to wear.

One of the day's most publicized activities was the butchering of the 1,000-pound Angus steer, provided by area cattle rancher Harvey Schmidt, fulfilling a bet he made with Pool earlier in the month. Schmidt had told Pool that, if Edgerton won the state tournament, he'd provide the meat for the victory celebration. So, early Monday morning he selected a steer, loaded it on his truck and delivered it to Main Street by 10:00 a.m. Pool took care of the shooting and skinning, and then suspended the beef from a front end tractor loader for all to see. As a bonus, he wrote the names of the players on the outer tallow.

The act in a later era almost would certainly have incited the wrath of People for the Ethical Treatment of Animals, but it served handsomely to provide for Edgerton's mother of all barbecues. The unfortunate steer, however, was not the source of the day's

Harvey Schmidt (right) contributed a 1,000-pound steer on a lost bet, and, along with Adrian Bouma, ceremoniously hung the beef on Main Street.

main course. The meat was taken to a local meat locker and exchanged for half a ton of cured beef.

Schmidt's loss was a major gain for Nick and Margaret Vlietstra, who had just purchased the Edgerton Home Bakery. On their first day of ownership, they received an early morning order for 3,000 buns and a hundred loaves of bread. The majority of residents were involved, donating pop, coffee, ice cream, and paper goods. The Leader and Spot cafes volunteered their cooking facilities to prepare the food and beverages, and there was no shortage of volunteers ready to serve the celebrants.

Bands from Leota, Jasper, Magnolia, Luverne, Worthington, and Ellsworth schools joined the celebration, along with several thousand out-of-town well-wishers and curiosity seekers.

By noon, everything was in order. Main Street was squeaky clean and decorated, the food was prepared, and in addition to Edgerton, the fleet of visiting bands were ready to perform. The town was packed with spectators, local and visitors, some perched on Main Street roofs. Long lines of cars were parked along roadways leading into town. Estimates of the crowd ranged from five to ten thousand. Among the visitors were familiar regular-season foes, including Coach Hugo Goehle from Hills and Lee Visker from Ellsworth. Magnolia's highly recruited athlete, Lloyd

Superintendent Bill Fure (forefront) guided off-court activities.

Voss, marched in his school band, playing the saxophone.

All that was missing were the Dutchmen and their coaches. Their estimated time of arrival was 2:00 p.m., but no one had any idea how many interruptions they would have between Minneapolis and Edgerton. A month earlier, many in Minnesota had never heard of Edgerton, and those who had paid little or no attention to the tiny Dutch community, but suddenly people from Warroad to Windom and points in between were discussing Edgerton. As the Dutchmen made their way toward home, residents in southern Minnesota lined their main streets and roads to catch a glimpse of the reigning state champions. From Minneapolis, the three-car Dutchmen cavalcade made a circuitous route that included stops in New Ulm, Redwood Falls, Pipestone, and Ruthton, although Redwood Falls wasn't on the original itinerary.

"Someone, around New Ulm, asked me when we planned to go through Redwood Falls, and I said that we weren't going to Redwood Falls," Fure said. "They told me, 'Well, you better go there because they are expecting you.'"

George Ramseth, Redwood Falls' school principal, had no authorization to dismiss classes for a welcoming party, so he scheduled a fire drill, and students lined the town's main street while George Mattson, Redwood County sheriff, escorted the Dutchmen through town.

Then, it was on to Marshall, Russell, Ruthton, and Pipestone, where Pipestone Mayor Roy Lee presented Olson with a pipestone peace pipe, symbolic of the town's name and perhaps a playful gesture demonstrating that its residents harbored no ill will for having the Arrows state tournament hopes dashed by the Dutchmen.

At 3:32 p.m., according to a *Worthington Globe* account, the team was greeted by a fire engine outside of town and the players jumped on the vehicle's standing rails and

After arriving home, the Dutchmen are loaded on an Edgerton fire truck for a parade.

were led into town by a highway patrol car. When they came onto Main Street—sirens blaring and church bells ringing—their admirers greeted them with a jubilant ovation. They were two hours late, but in Edgerton's history, never had so few received such an enthusiastic welcome from so many. The bands had begun an impromptu parade, but were abruptly disbanded when the crowd began to swarm the fire engine.

"It was an emotional experience and fun, but the trip

seemed to take forever," Veenhof said. "It was a lot more fun when we got home because we were in familiar territory. We didn't know anyone in Minneapolis or in the towns along the way."

Slowly, the players and coaches reached the presentation stand and made their way onto the stage on which designated master of ceremonies Bertus Kooiman, an Edgerton senior when the school basketball team last won twenty games, made several brief statements and then turned the program over to Olson and his players. Each was asked to describe the highlight of his week.

Darrell Kreun had been enjoying the festivities until then, but the guard who demonstrated a calm and commanding presence before at least 18,000 fans in three state tournament games, suddenly developed a major case of stage fright.

"We figured there was going to be some sort of celebration in the gym, but we never imagined so many people would turn out," Kreun said. "If I had known we were going to be asked to speak, I might have found a way to sneak off. That was not my cup of tea."

Olson, often mistaken for a player because of his youthful appearance, playfully groused that Graphenteen kept pointing at him and telling people how he was actually a starting Dutchmen forward. Veenhof, the team's resident chow hound, evoked a collective laugh when he revealed that next to winning the championship, the most enjoyable part of his week was the Curtis hotel food.

After the comments, several Edgerton students performed playful skits, with Eric Vanderbush—a future National Merit Scholar—temporarily stealing the show with his theatrical rechristening of Olson.

Dressed in Dutch garb, the bespectacled senior had

Rich Olson is converted into "official" Dutchman on Main Street while a crowd estimated at between 5,000 and 10,000 observe the ceremony.

Olson stand up, and raising his right hand over the Scandinavian coach's head proclaimed: "You are no longer a Norwegian. You are now a Dutchman. You are a Flying Dutchman. You are an Edgerton Flying Dutchman. You are now christened 'Reinhart Van Olson.'"

Once the ceremony ended, a robust feast began and continued late into the afternoon and early evening. Thousands of barbeques and thousands of bottles of pop, donated by the Pepsi Cola Company, were consumed . . . although the coach and his wife were too busy accepting congratulations to enjoy a bite of the beef.

Daryl Stevens, Edgerton's top reserve, remembers

the melancholy that came near the end. "People were starting to leave, and I'm thinking, 'Hey, guys, the party isn't over,'" he said. "Then suddenly, I remember my dad coming up to me and saying, 'It's time to go . . . we've got cows to milk.' That was really a letdown."

The celebration ended that evening, but the town

John and Sally Rath (left) and Rich and Maryls Olson take a well-deserved break during the post-season tournament celebration.

later threw the players a championship dinner, as did many other towns far and near throughout the spring. In one of Marlys Olson's scrapbooks, the coach's wife compiled a list of fourteen out-of-town banquets in which the Dutchmen were featured guests, from as near as Luverne, Ruthton, and Pipestone and as distant as Moorhead, Owatonna, and both Minneapolis and St. Paul.

"It seemed as if every Friday night, Ole would load us in his car, and off we'd go to some banquet," Veenhof said.

"I don't remember learning much that last couple of months of school," added Kreun.

Meanwhile, a deluge of congratulatory cards and let-

Basketball was on the minds of most, but education remained a priority.

ters poured into Fure's and Olson's mailboxes, praising them for their leadership and their players' exemplary conduct, on and off the court. The *Enterprise* received letters applauding the team and the town, with many requesting copies of the newspaper's post-tournament coverage. A couple from Madison, South Dakota, said that Edgerton's successful state championship bid attracted almost as much interest as did the results of South Dakota's State A and B tournaments. Pastors from Paynesville and Long Lake, first a Lutheran minister and the other an Assembly of God clergyman, expressed their appreciation for the team's respect for the Sabbath.

"In contrast to the official welcome Wayzata received last year on Sunday morning (thus making local residents choose between the natural desire to honor the athletes and church worship), these young Christian men from Edgerton went to church, as is their usual custom on Sunday," wrote Pastor Vriesman from Long Lake's Trinity Lutheran Church.

As for the players, although only a junior, Dean Veenhof—one of the state's most publicized centers—attracted the most recruiting interest. Dean Verdoes, the team leader and honor student, received a number of academic inquiries, although he already had been accepted and was committed to Macalester on an academic scholarship. And LeRoy Graphenteen, described by one Minneapolis columnist as "a bouncy, talky, gum-chewing little half pint" was the most popular Dutchman player, particularly among star-struck girls, ages eleven through eighteen.

Graphenteen received more than one hundred letters inquiring if he had a girlfriend, asking if had a car and what kind, telling him to write, call, or even visit if he was interested, and informing him that he was an extremely cute guy who probably could date anyone he chose. Many of the letters began, "I know you'll think I am crazy for writing, but . . ."

Graphenteen said he responded to a few, but ultimately married a Pipestone woman who wasn't even remotely smitten by the diminutive guard who helped defeat her school's Arrow basketball team.

And finally, there was the rumor mill in which Olson's coaching future was a popular topic. The rumors began flying during tournament week, understandably considering his success at such a young age, and they continued to do so through the spring. Olson said that Sid Hartman, the venerable *Minneapolis Star-Tribune*'s sports columnist, seemed to have Olson headed somewhere every week. Ted Peterson, the *Star-Tribune* high school sports-

> March 29, 1960
>
> Dear LeRoy Graphenteen
>   I am a very devoted fan
> of yours I'm 14 years old I'm 5'7"
> and I'm in the ninth grade at
> Sanford Jr high. My favorite
> subjects are Math and Gym.
> My favorite sports are baseball and
> basketball but I guess I like all
> sports. I think you play basketball
> just great. You were the best player
> on the team. Really I guess every body
> was good But I wrote to you because
> I liked you the best I also like Dean
> Veenhof and Dean Vurdoes.
>   I would like you to please send
> me an autographed picture of yourself.
> I would like to know when your
> birthday is? how old are you? what
> are your favorite subjects in school
> I just thought I would write to
> you and let you know I was and
> still am a devoted fan

LeRoy Graphenteen enjoyed rock-star adulation from girls statewide. The Edgerton guard received approximately 100 letters from teen girls.

writer, revealed that Olson had received "six or seven offers" after the tournament, but said Olson was staying in Edgerton for at least another year.

Peterson was correct. In the spring, when the

Enterprise annually reported names of the school faculty leaving, Olson's name was not on the list, and when school was dismissed for the summer he immediately resumed his duties as the town's recreational director. He perhaps saw some excellent coaching and teaching opportunities throughout the state, some with significantly loftier salaries, but it seemed that money couldn't buy a better situation than the one he had in Edgerton.

Dutchmen admire the hard-earned hardware on display at Jolinks.

CHAPTER TEN
The Years After

While the excitement gradually diminished, the alley basketball games continued through the summer and into the fall for Edgerton's reigning state champions, but come basketball season, three of the major players in the improbable journey were gone. Dean Verdoes was in St. Paul, enrolled at Macalester College. Bob Wiarda was in Sioux City, Iowa, attending Morningside College. And Daryl Stevens was just down the road in Worthington Junior College.

Wiarda, Stevens, and Verdoes were all part of the previous season's Dutchmen football team, but their absence appeared to have little impact on the season which for Edgerton ended 6 and 1 with the lone loss to Hills 27 to 18 on the Blue Jays' homecoming. Quarterback Darrell Kreun was the team's leading scorer with fifty-seven points and earned honorable mention on the Minnesota All-State Eight-Man team. Dean Veenhof, a starting end, was one of sixteen first-team all-state selections, earning him the rare distinction of being an all-state player in two sports.

"I think that my basketball reputation had more to do with my being selected than my football ability," the 6-foot-5 Veenhof said.

Beyond the University of Minnesota's 1960 outlook, football became a moot subject in and around Edgerton after the team's final snap. High school basketball—Flying Dutchmen basketball in particular—became the major source of conversation. From Edgerton to Luverne and Slayton to Minneapolis, the speculation was not whether Edgerton would be good, but rather would the Dutchmen be good enough to win another state championship. The Dutchmen had three returning all-tournament players from a team that won twenty-seven straight games, a winning streak led by all-state center Veenhof, sharp-shooting guard Kreun, and tenacious defender and deft ball-handler LeRoy Graphenteen. Veenhof had gained twenty pounds, Graphenteen grew two inches to 5-foot-10, and Kreun had another eight months to refine his amazing shooting touch.

In addition, 6-foot-2 Jim Roos, the previous season's top reserve who missed the tournament with a broken arm, was expected to help ease the losses at forward while 6-foot-4 Bob Dykstra and 6-foot-1 Larry Schoolmeester were contending for the other front-court vacancy.

LeRoy Graphenteen, Darrel Kreun, and Dean Veenhof were Edgerton's tri-captains for the 1960-1961 Flying Dutchmen basketball team.

"We went at it like we were going to do it again . . . that was our goal, to get back [to the state tournament]," Olson said. "We knew that we didn't have everything that we had the year before, having replaced two starting forwards, but when you've got a good center and two good guards, that's an excellent start."

Of obvious concern was the lack of depth. The remainder of his roster, including Dykstra and Schoolmeester, spent the majority of the previous season on the "B" team and, with the exception of Schoolmeester's two and one-half intense minutes in the epic Richfield game, had no quality varsity experience. Sophomores Bob Westenberg and Doug Schelhaas and freshmen Vernon Schoolmeester, Jake Kooiman, and Bernie Stoel would be major players in Edgerton's future, but none was deemed ready for even reserve duty. This made Norm Prins, a 6-foot-4 standout at the Christian School, all the more alluring to Olson and Flying Dutchmen fans.

"He would have made a huge difference," said Kreun, who played a season with Prins at Northwestern College in Orange City, Iowa. "If we had had him, we would have had an even better chance than we did to win [the state title] again."

In fact, a rumor surfaced during that summer that Prins was headed to the public school. The farm kid from near Leota played on Edgerton's American Legion baseball team, coached by Olson and which included many of his players. Prins said he fancied the idea of playing basketball with the public school, but said he and his parents never discussed the possibility of his transferring, and Olson never attempted to recruit him. George Schelhaas, a 6-foot sophomore, did transfer from Southwestern Christian to Edgerton's public school, but Prins remained at SWC and led them to a Tri-State Conference title.

"In my heart I thought how neat it would be to play on a team like they had," Prins said. "But also in my heart, I knew how much it would hurt my parents. My father was a member of the [Christian] school board and my aunts and uncles had been instrumental in the organization of the school. I was a compliant son. I did what my parents considered to be the right thing.

"The same thing went for Leon Fey. He probably could have helped as much as I might have. He was a good player, an excellent scorer and ball handler, and he also stayed at the Christian School. I think we both scored more than 1,000 points while we were there."

Bruce Timmer, Southwest Christian's leading scorer the year before, moved to California, but the Eagles finished 16 and 4 and won the Inter-State Academy Conference title, led by Prins and his 20.7 scoring average.

The 17 and 4 Southwest Christian team might have been a good match for 1960-1961 Dutchmen. Members were (left) Larry Van Essen, Bill Vande Pol, Arvin Schaap, Curtis Pool, Daryl Baar, Norm Prins, Ken Vos, Leon Fey, Willy Vander Pol, Curt Pals. Prins, who played one more season, wound up as the Christian School's all-time scorer with 1,066 points.

EDGERTON

Edgerton began the season with a revised schedule. The Dutchmen played a home-and-home Tri-County schedule, but bumped one game from each of their perennial two-game sets against both Chandler and Jasper to make room for road games against Bloomington and Minneapolis Roosevelt, the latter a preliminary to the Gophers' non-conference game against St. Mary's of California. The two Twin Cities-area opponents, along with big-school dates against Slayton and Luverne, were the foundation to what was unquestionably the toughest schedule ever faced by an Edgerton team.

"We've won twenty-seven straight, but I'm sure we're going to have a lot tougher going this season," Olson said at the Moorhead clinic, one of his many off-season appearances. "We play at Bloomington on November 26 and face Roosevelt in Williams Arena in late December. Both of those will be severe tests, and Luverne will be big and strong and the team to beat in our district."

Edgerton began the previous season as little more than one of 488 state public schools to field a basketball team, but the new band of Flying Dutchmen and their second-year leader were preseason fodder for not only the *Enterprise* and *Worthington Globe*, but for most of the state daily newspapers including the *Minneapolis Star-Tribune*. Ted Peterson, the *Star-Tribune*'s veteran high school sportswriter, set the bar high for Edgerton when he compared the team's challenge to Buhl, the last small-town basketball champion to successfully defend its state title in 1942, but the Dutchmen needed no outside motivation to prepare.

"I think we were all feeling some pressure," Veenhof said. "We knew that we had lost two good players in Verdoes and Wiarda and although we figured we'd be all right within our league, the Bloomington and Roosevelt games were a concern. It still was fun, and we enjoyed ourselves, but it was different than the year before when we were on a high and blowing people out."

Verdoes was the major loss, not only because of his court skills, but also because of his leadership and calming influence in difficult situations, particularly when opponents applied full-court pressure. But one shouldn't understate Wiarda's values, often not reflected in box scores. The muscular forward did not score a great deal, but he was fierce on the boards and knew how to get the ball to Veenhof.

Coach Rich Olson (left) with 1960-1961 Flying Dutchmen Dean Veenhof, Bob Dykstra, Larry Schoolmeester, Jim Roos, Norm Muilenburg, Doug Schelhaas, Ken Koster, Larry Stevens, Bob Westenberg, LeRoy Graphenteen, Darrell Kreun, Tom Warren, and Bob Baker.

On November 25, Edgerton began its new season defeating Adrian with ease, 83 to 41, at home where Veenhof scored twenty-seven, Kreun twenty-five, and Roos had ten in his first varsity start. The next day the Flying Dutchmen carried their twenty-eight game winning streak to the Twin Cities area where they played a night game against Bloomington, one of the two Lake Conference schools to beat Richfield the previous season. Coach Don Snyder lost all his starters from a 12 and 6 season, but Dean Wolbrink—son of the former Edgerton minister and a Bloomington student—sensed that the team's leader was confident.

"He knew I was from Edgerton since the team had been to our church the Sunday after winning the state championship," Wolbrink said. "He and I met in the hall one day not long before the game, and I asked, 'Do you think we can beat them?' He had a quiet nature and was a secure individual and simply said, 'We'll see,' but to me there was a twinkle in his eye that indicated he thought there would be no contest."

A contest there was, but Don Snyder's Bloomington Bears were no match for the country crowd in the end. Edgerton led by only one point at the intermission, but outscored Bloomington by eleven in the third quarter and coasted to a 67 to 60 romp before a capacity crowd. The Dutchmen answer the first major question regarding their ability to repeat. The Bears would go on to finish second to Edina in the Lake Conference.

"Bloomington was a big game," Veenhof said of the game in which he scored twenty-nine points matched against 6-foot-7 center Dennis Allaman. "Once we won, I think we expected that we had an outstanding chance of getting back to the tournament and winning it."

In the next three weeks, the Dutchmen ran their winning streak to thirty-two consecutive victories, defeating Lake Wilson, Ellsworth, and Hills by a combined margin of seventy-three points. Ellsworth was a 45 to 35 decision in which Edgerton led by only three points before pulling away in the fourth quarter. After four games, Dykstra had secured the fifth starting spot, with reserve duties shared by Larry Schoolmeester, Norm Muilenburg, and Darwin Fey. Dykstra perhaps solidified his starting spot in Edgerton's 73 to 54 victory over Hills, coached by the crafty Hugo Goehle.

"We let Bob Dykstra go in the first half so we could defend against Dean Veenhof," Goehle explained. "But Dykstra killed us with fourteen points in that half."

Next stop was Williams Arena in what was a curtain call of sorts, but also an enormous challenge. The opponent was Roosevelt, a perennial Minneapolis City League team that won back-to-back state titles in 1956 and 1957 and was a major contender to replace Edgerton as state champion. Before what *Sioux Falls Argus-Leader* sportswriter John Egan described as probably "the largest crowd" ever to attend a Gopher preliminary game. Roosevelt defeated the Dutchmen 66 to 58, ending their winning streak in wire-to-wire fashion. If the Dutchmen seniors had forgotten how much the 1959 District 8 loss to Jasper hurt, they experienced a woeful reminder.

Edgerton shot poorly, and 6-foot-3 center Fred Warn contained Veenhof in a first half that ended with Roosevelt leading 38 to 23. Warn fouled out with five minutes left in the third quarter and Veenhof led an Edgerton rally, but Roosevelt coach C. Wayne Courtney countered with stall tactics, and Edgerton ran out of time to the dismay of many in the large crowd.

"It was devastating," Veenhof said. "Fred Warn was tough and did a good job of fronting me, but it was a major letdown because we knew we hadn't played well."

Adding insult to injury was Courtney's harsh postgame remarks. The outspoken coach began innocently enough, telling the Twin Cities press corps that his team was mentally prepared and attributed the victory to rebounding superiority, a well-executed full-court press, and Warn's job of fronting Veenhof in the first sixteen minutes.

Then came Courtney's harsh assessment of the Dutchmen, past and present. His comments were controversial and bordered on contempt. He named three other Minneapolis city conference teams—and added a possible fourth—which would have beaten Edgerton on this night, and said that his previous season's Teddies would have defeated the 1960 state champion Dutchmen. "I didn't think they were a super team last year," he said, "and I'm convinced they aren't now."

Edgerton played one more game before the holiday break, defeating Magnolia 87 to 39 and twenty-one days later opened the New Year by breaking the school's single-game scoring record in a 102-to-57 victory over Beaver Creek. Veenhof scored a season-high thirty-four points, one of five double-figure totals for the Dutchmen. Courtney may not have had any respect for Edgerton, but statewide high school basketball pundit Art Johlfs did by placing the Dutchmen sixth in a mid-season poll behind Austin, Bemidji, Minneapolis Roosevelt, Duluth Central, Minneapolis Southwest and ahead of Willmar, Anoka, Thief River Falls, and St. Paul Central.

"A team can lose a game or two and still be the best in the state, at least until tournament time when upsets are a dime a dozen," Johlfs said. "Despite predictions of defeat for doughty little Edgerton, they scored 102 points in a recent game, proving the power of three all-state players and a decent team."

The Magnolia and Beaver Creek victories were the beginning of an eleven-game winning streak leading up to their final regular-season game against Luverne. The

Dutchmen completed an undefeated Tri-County season for the second year, capped by a fifty-three-point victory over Adrian on the road, and defeated Slayton by twenty-seven points despite the Wildcats' attempt to control the ball from the outset.

Each February since the mid-fifties, Edgerton and Luverne had met in what was the final regular-season game for both and in recent years an intense neighborhood rivalry had evolved. This season's meeting, however, couldn't have been more intense. The Flying Dutchmen and Cardinals were both 16 and 1, champions of their respective conferences, and arguably co-favorites in the upcoming District 8 tournament. Luverne, similar to Edgerton, lost early in the season, a 65 to 63 setback at Windom where the Cardinals' hit their last shot, but it was ruled to have been taken a split second too late to force overtime. The teams each had a gifted big man, 6-foot-5 Veenhof for Edgerton and 6-foot-3 Andy Hagemann for Luverne, and Edgerton's Olson and Luverne's Bob Erdman were two of the state's most respected coaches.

Fan interest surpassed the Luverne gymnasium's 2,400-seat capacity, and the game was a sellout long before the Friday night tip-off. So intense was the Friday night fever that the Luverne Junior Chamber of Conference rented a sixteen-foot screen from Sioux City, Iowa, and placed it in the high school theater, which seated approximately 500 additional spectators. Veenhof said that, after the loss against Roosevelt, he thought "nothing could be as exciting as the year before," but the 1961 Edgerton-Luverne game was one of the series' all-time thrillers.

In a physical contest cluttered by fifty fouls, Luverne defeated Edgerton 68 to 66. Luverne led by three points at the half, but Edgerton came back to take a 50 to 49 advantage into the final quarter despite the fourteen-minute absence of Veenhof, who picked up three quick personals in the first quarter and was pulled two minutes into the second quarter after being called for a fourth personal. The center started the fourth quarter, but less than two minutes into the quarter he picked up his fifth personal and exited with only one more point than fouls.

The game, however, would be remembered best for two things, one being Darrell Kreun's incredible one-man show throughout the losing cause which ended with three Dutchmen on the bench, and the other being the game's quirky ending.

Darrell Kreun had a career night in a regular-season loss to Luverne.

Kreun didn't win the game, but he won respect from both sides with his play, particularly down the stretch when he and Bob Dykstra were the only Dutchmen starters on the floor. Unable to contain Kreun for most of the game, the absence of Veenhof, Graphenteen, and Roos enabled the Luverne defense to focus on the diminutive guard. He stepped up in the end with a pair of free throws and a field goal that tied the game at 66 with nine seconds left, his thirty-eight points only three shy of his career high in a far less important game a year earlier.

"It was one of the most amazing performances I've ever seen," Southwest Christian star Norm Prins said of Kreun, who three games earlier had quietly surpassed the

1,000-point career scoring mark against Chandler. "They had two guys on him, and he still was hitting from everywhere."

Kreun's field goal tied the game with less than ten seconds left, but the Cardinals turned to their star, who quickly drove toward the basket and lofted a last-second shot. He missed the field-goal attempt, but was fouled by Kreun and calmly sank a pair of free throws with no time left. Hagemann finished with thirty-five points, going fifteen for eighteen from the line.

"I remember that I pretty much kept us in the game and that it felt sort of a hopeless cause out there with so many players missing," Kreun said. "You hate to lose your final game going into the tournament, but we sort of looked at the loss as a fluke because we didn't really show what we were capable of doing as a team."

Edgerton ravaged Beaver Creek 80 to 59 to open its District 8 title defense, but the Dutchmen didn't barge through the remaining games with the irresistible force they had a year earlier. Hills, a team Edgerton defeated by forty-six points less than a month earlier, trailed by only four points with four minutes to go before the Dutchmen pulled away to a 71 to 58 victory, another tribute to the wily Hugo Goehle. In a journeyman effort, Edgerton defeated Worthington 70 to 56, setting up a classic rematch against Luverne.

In front of 3,300 spectators in the Worthington gymnasium, plus a closed-circuit audience of 300 in the school cafeteria, the Cardinals and Dutchmen exchanged leads or shared ties on more than a dozen occasions, before Edgerton claimed a 58 to 49 decision on what was the second straight joyous St. Patrick's Day for the Dutch community.

Happy Flying Dutchmen players beat Luverne in the District 8 final, avenging their regular-season loss to the highly ranked Cardinals.

"I thought we had them a couple times," an emotional Luverne coach Bob Erdman said in his post-game remarks. "My kids were doing a fine job, but Edgerton is a great team and real champions. They keep the pressure on you all the time. Just one mistake and bang, it's over."

In the Region II tournament, also played at Worthington, Edgerton was the only returnee from the previous season. The Dutchmen were paired against Wells, 18 and 2, whose only losses were to Minneapolis Patrick Henry and Fairmont, while Jackson, 16 and 5, was paired against St. James, 17 and 4.

Jackson defeated Okabena in the District 7 final after Okabena eliminated perennial power Mountain Lake. Wells defeated Ceylon, the only team to beat Okabena in the regular season, in District 5. And arguably the most surprising regional entrant was St. James, who en route to the District 6 title defeated three-time defending champion Mankato in the semifinals.

"We had basically the same team back for my senior year, and we were favored to get back to the state tournament," Mankato's Leroy Schweim said. "But we didn't even get out of the district. We got beat in a close game by St. James, who we beat during the regular season. We were looking past them to Edgerton because we wanted so badly to get back at them for the previous season."

Before another capacity crowd in Worthington, Edgerton rolled 75 to 63 over Wells, coached by the venerable Lloyd Stuessy, who was completing his nineteenth season at Wells and his twenty-third season overall. The Wildcats trailed by only five at the half, but Edgerton held them scoreless in the first four and one-half minutes of the third quarter and pulled away. Darrell Kreun scored twenty-four and put the game out of reach with a twelve-point fourth-quarter spree.

"They tried a zone press on us, but Darrell just kept coming down, hitting the brakes and hitting jump shot after jump shot," Olson said. "He was a tremendous outside shooter. I wonder how many points he would have scored if the three-point line had been in. He probably would have averaged at least six or seven more points a game. Nobody shot it better."

Jackson, playing what its coach Dave Berger described as "our best by far," defeated St. James 70 to 64 in the other Region II semifinal, and the Blue Jays put together an excellent opening half against Edgerton. The Dutchmen, struggling offensively, led by only one after sixteen minutes, but the Flying Dutchmen took flight behind Veenhof who finished with thirty-two points in a 65 to 52 victory that made Edgerton only the fourth team in Region II history to successfully repeat at least once.

Edgerton celebrated but not with the gusto of the year before when the Dutchmen vaulted from obscurity into the spotlight they shared with the recent U.S. Olympic hockey champions. The welcome home didn't go into the wee hours of the next morning, and it was very much a business-as-usual atmosphere on Main Street. Even the media, which the year before converged on the village and chronicled the country kids' every move, was far more conservative in its coverage of Edgerton this time. The only constant was another marathon scouting trip by Olson, who on the Saturday before state tournament week drove to Grand Forks, North Dakota, where Bemidji defeated Halstad 74 to 45 to claim the Region VIII title and state tournament matchup against Edgerton.

"It was not one of [Coach Bun Fortier's] best state tournament teams," longtime *Bemidji Tribune* sportswriter Jim Carrington said of the Bemidji Lumberjacks, who had a record of 20 and 3 entering the state competition, "but they were what I'd call over achievers who played well together."

If Olson believed the Lumberjacks had so-so talent, he certainly didn't share his opinion with the team.

Mahtomedi, Duluth Central, Winona, Sauk Centre, Minneapolis Roosevelt, and Danube joined the Dutchmen and Bemidji in the tournament field. Edgerton still had some charm, a carry-over from its improbable 1960 state tournament championship run, but tiny Danube, population 494, was the tournament sweetheart.

Still, no one was overlooking the Dutchmen's chances of repeating, but the consensus favorite was 24 and 0 Duluth Central, a team averaging fifty-two percent from the floor. The Trojans had its entire team back from the previous season when Central, with a 19 and 0 record was upset by Duluth Morgan Park in District 26. Central had an outstanding inside-outside combination with 6-foot-3 sophomore Chet Anderson and 6-foot-1 guard Terry Kunze.

Deemed to be a major contender was Region V champion Minneapolis Roosevelt, winner of twenty-two consecutive games since its lone loss to De La Salle, the eventual 1961 State Catholic League champion. Edgerton and Roosevelt were in the same bracket, and, if both won their openers, they would meet in the semifinals, generating anticipation of a heated rematch in light of Coach Wayne Courtney's critical critique of Edgerton basketball in December.

The media, perhaps buoyed by prospects of controversy, asked Olson if he and his players would like another shot at the Teddies, but the Edgerton coach—still irate about Courtney's remarks—refused to take the bait, telling writers that Bemidji was the team's only concern. In an earlier interview, he said that Luverne, not Roosevelt, was the toughest team Edgerton had played during the season, and years later he insisted that his response was not an intended jab at Courtney.

"That's really what I thought," he said. "The Twin Cities schools always thought they had the best teams, but the out-state schools had some excellent teams, too. I thought we had proved that the year before."

Olson had every reason to respect the Luverne Cardinals. They defeated Edgerton in the regular season and were led by Hagemann, one of the most respected players in the state.

The speculation, however, became moot long before Edgerton took the floor on Thursday night against the Lumberjacks. In one of state tournament history's most controversial decisions, Minnesota State High School League officials disqualified Roosevelt for having used two ineligible players, an action that wound up in a district court before the league's decision was upheld by a pair of judges.

If the league's action had been based on a legal or academic violation, the ruling might have been readily accepted, but the issue involved Warren Scamp and John Totushek, a pair of reserves whose tournament participation had been limited to seconds. They reportedly had participated in an unsanctioned basketball activity the previous spring, a violation of a league rule that prohibited athletes with varsity eligibility from formal off-season competition in the sport for which they were eligible. Courtney's plight evoked sympathy from his coaching peers, the media, and fans, but the judges upheld the rule.

What some considered to be Courtney's best team since Roosevelt won back to back in 1956 and 1957, perhaps even better than those teams, lost the biggest court battle of an outstanding season. Even some of the outspoken Courtney's major detractors had to experience some of his pain.

Almost as controversial was the choice of Roosevelt's replacement in the eight-team field. Royalton was 19 and 4, but were defeated by the Teddies 70 to 59 in the Region V semifinals. Mound was ousted 62 to 55 by Roosevelt in the Region V final and was given no credit for its 47 to 30 semifinal victory over Atwater and its narrower margin of defeat. Royalton beat Mound for a state tournament spot by virtue of a coin flip, though no announcement was made whether Royalton had heads or tails. Perhaps the Mound team and its coach uttered a quiet "I told you so" when Royalton—a team that had not practiced all week—lost its opener to Winona by twenty points.

Courtney showed some class in his meeting with Roosevelt students, faculty, and parents by telling them that no matter how disillusioned they were by the decision, not to do anything that would reflect unfavorably upon the school. Addressing the media, he said: "I thought there would be some room for mercy in the board decision. It didn't work out that way. The board was convinced it acted properly, and perhaps it did. But they will not be able to walk away from this. Some will have sleepless nights."

It would be a sleepless Thursday night for Edgerton's defending state champions after losing to Bemidji, 76 to 67, in the opening round—Coach Bun Fortier's first opening-game victory in six state tourney trips since 1954. Veenhof fouled out with two minutes and thirty-three seconds left in the third quarter, and while his Edgerton teammates were not unaccustomed to playing without the foul-prone center, they couldn't do what they did a year earlier against Richfield. The Dutchmen trailed by eleven points in the fourth quarter and managed to pare the margin to five on several occasions, but each time Bemidji answered the challenge.

Although Bemidji shot only 39.8 percent from the floor, Olson blamed a lackluster

Not even Darrell Kreun's silky touch could help Edgerton defend it's state title.

defense that yielded more than seventy points for the first time since he had become head coach; in fact, only five teams managed to score more than sixty points against Edgerton in Olson's first two seasons. Veenhof scored twenty-one points in his abbreviated appearance, but Bemidji's Larry Higgins had twenty-six and Jack Phelps had twenty-two.

"Before the game, I told our kids that we would have to keep our hands up and play them tight," Olson said. "We did neither. We gave Bemidji easy shots, and they took advantage. Sure, we could have used Veenhof in the last quarter, but it was our defense which hurt us the most."

Bemidji stirred up many "what ifs" for Edgerton in the next two nights. The Lumberjacks defeated Winona 57 to 51 in the semifinals, overcoming an eleven-point deficit, and in a 51 to 50 loss to Duluth Central for the championship, Bemidji's Lee Fawbush took a twelve-foot base-line jumper that rolled around the rim and spun out.

In the consolation bracket, a sluggish Edgerton muddled through a 66 to 58 victory over Royalton, trailing by two in the fourth quarter before showing signs of life. In the consolation final, Edgerton played another lackluster game and lost to Mahtomedi 51 to 49. The score was tied, and Edgerton had the ball with less than a minute remaining, but turned the ball over and with two seconds left, 6-foot-6 center Mike Patterson drove past Veenhof on the baseline and scored the winning basket.

"I think we were flat," Kreun said of the tournament. "All of our senior year we just thought about returning to the state tournament, and when we got there we just didn't seem to have it."

Olson was upset by his team's loss to Bemidji and was equally disappointed by their play in the remaining two games, but he made no excuses for the overall Flying Dutchmen season. He was proud that they returned to the state tournament, emphasizing that the task was far more difficult the second year.

"The first year we were treated like heroes coming back from the Twin Cities, but the second year everybody was out to get us," he said. "We were even egged a couple times, once in Chandler where we had to have someone watch our bus during the game, and the other time in one of the bigger towns down there."

Rumors surfaced once again in post-season that Olson might leave Edgerton. Hopkins and Robbinsdale, two Twin Cities suburban schools with far more athletic depth and higher pay scales showed the greatest interest in the young coach with a 50 and 4 career record and back-to-back state tournament appearances. The time seemed right for Olson to move on, but he remained to deal with an imposing building season.

"Things had been going well at Edgerton, and my wife was able to teach," he said. "I figured I'd stay at least one more year and maybe get a better offer. I was also looking at colleges, but back then they didn't pay what they do today to tackle a major rebuilding task."

Gone now were all five members of the 1960 state championship team and the four starters from his 1961 state tournament team: Veenhof (1,887 career points), Kreun (1,268 points), playmaker and defensive ace Graphenteen, and the steady Roos. Olson began with one starter in Bob Dykstra and sixth man Larry Schoolmeester, a pair of forwards. The remaining three starters and top reserves would have to be selected from an inexperienced group of varsity returnees and the B team.

Senior Darwin Fey missed his junior season because of a football injury and figured in the equation, but the

Coach Rich Olson rebuilt the Edgerton lineup in 1961-1962. Members were Vern "Tonto" Schoolmeester, D.J. Fey, Larry Schoolmeester, Bernie Stoel, and Bob Dykstra.

most exciting prospect was Vernon Schoolmeester, leading scorer on the previous season's 13 and 1 B team. Schoolmeester, second cousin of Larry Schoolmeester, was cut from the same cloth as the coach and the 1960 state championship squad, a quintessential gym rat with tremendous athletic ability and an intense passion for basketball. Schoolmeester, however, insisted that he wasn't alone when it came to a love of the game.

"We had a bunch of kids who wanted to play," he said. "I remember me and four, five, six guys going to Ole's place on a Saturday night and him giving us the key to the gym. We'd put on a Gopher-Ohio State game, or something like that, and we'd go up and down the court for hours. We were all very much into it."

Schoolmeester was a full-time B team player, but occasionally dressed for the varsity games and was on the 1961 tournament roster. Olson was aware of Schoolmeester's promise long before the season began but didn't believe the skinny 5-foot-6 guard was ready for varsity competition. Certainly, his chances for varsity playing time would have been limited with two thirty-two minute all-state guards in the lineup. Olson did place Schoolmeester on the tournament roster, recognizing that he had matured and believing that the youngster's ball-handling ability and court sense could be insurance should he encounter foul or injury problems in the backcourt. As for Schoolmeester, he said he never questioned the coach's early season decision to leave him on the B team.

"I was developing into a good player, but because of my lack of height and strength, I was definitely not ready," Schoolmaster said, "As I look back, I feel fortunate to have watched those older guys develop and accomplish what they did . . . to have also interacted with them and learned so much from them."

Edgerton's rebuilding season had its frustrations, but it wasn't as imposing as Olson had anticipated, in large part to the now 5-foot-10 Schoolmeester's growth and progress and 6-foot-3 Bernie Stoel's significant improvement. On what would be a 14 and 5 season, Schoolmeester was the team's scoring leader with 313, and Stoel figured prominently with his post play and impressive ability to go outside. Edgerton lost to Magnolia, Jasper, Slayton, and Luverne in the regular season. The inexplicable 67 to 52 loss to Magnolia ended a thirty-seven Tri-County Conference winning streak—and the Flying Dutchmen were eliminated by Pipestone in their District 8 opener.

On the plus side, a relatively inexperienced Edgerton team won its first eleven games, claimed the Tri-County title with a 13 and 1 record, was undefeated at home, and Pipestone, the eventual District 8 champion needed a fourth-quarter rally in its 47 to 42 tourney victory over Edgerton as Arrows coach Ed Otto exacted an element of revenge for his 1960 tournament loss to the Flying Dutchmen. A side note is the fact that Edgerton had four of the better players in southwest Minnesota, but unfortunately 6-foot-4 Norm Prins and 6-foot Leon Fey played for Southwest Christian School, combining for 731 points.

"There was a lot of basketball talent scattered around Edgerton," said Bruce Timmer, another Christian School standout who transferred to California the season after his sophomore year and started for a school with an enrollment in the thousands. "The year they won, it was one of those things like 'Could I have played on that team?'"

In what would be his final season in Edgerton, Olson once again shunned off-season offers and guided Edgerton to its second perfect regular season in four years. The Flying Dutchmen swept their Tri-County schedule for a

The 1963 Dutchmen were undefeated through district play. Players included (left) Gene Fransen, Vern Schoolmeester, Bob Westenberg, Curt Pool, Doug Schelhaas, Bernie Stoel, B. Markl, Gene Boysen, Gary Loenhorst, Jake Kooiman, and Curt Vanderstoop. In front, are manager Arsene Schmidt, Coach Rich Olson, and Eddie Clark.

four-year 55 and 1 record and defeated non-conference foes Jasper, Slayton, and Luverne. The season's only brush with frustration was a 62 to 60 victory over Beaver Creek, an overtime decision sealed by Schoolmeester's twenty-five-foot jumper.

"We beat Luverne in the final [regular-season] game, and they had a good team," Schoolmeester said of an 81 to 68 victory. "We felt that we could play with anyone."

Entering the post-season, the town of Edgerton once again came to life, the players and townspeople anticipating another state tournament trip. The Dutchmen, being compared to the 1960 state championship team, inspired even greater expectations with an overwhelming District 8 performance concluded by a 58 to 49 victory over Luverne, and the town was described to be "a ghost town by 5:30" the evening of the Region II opener against St. James.

The starting lineup included Vernon Schoolmeester, Stoel, Kooiman, Bob Westenberg, and Doug Schelhaas, the latter a Christian School transfer two years earlier, with Gene Boysen and Curt Vanderstoop providing stellar role play. Beyond the 6-foot-3 Stoel, none of the starters or top reserves was

Gene Boysen pulls down a rebound against Luverne as Bernie Stoel and Bob Westenberg watch.

taller than 6-foot, but Stoel had matured into an excellent center, scoring a season-high forty points against Chandler, and anything seemed possible with the ubiquitous Schoolmeester on the court.

"I wasn't certain that we'd win the state again, but I really believed we were going back to the state tournament, I really did," Kooiman said. "I figured that if we played a normal game, we'd come out of the region. Bernie and Tonto [Schoolmeester's nickname] would score sixty percent of the points while Doug, Bob, and I would come up with the rest."

The Dutchmen appeared to receive a favorable draw in the region semifinals, pitted against a St. James team that was 11 and 6 entering District 6 play in which the Saints defeated Mankato, Madelia, and Waldorf-Pemberton. While a Region II final between Edgerton and Wells seemed likely, St. James defeated the Dutchmen 59 to 48 in one of the state's major upsets.

Schoolmeester had an excellent game, scoring twenty-seven points, but Stoel—the team's leading scorer—hit only three of seventeen field goal attempts, and the usually steady Kooiman had almost as many fouls as he did points. Kooiman vividly remembers being pulled by Olson, irate because of the forward's failure to box out, and making

Jake Kooiman, Bernie Stoel, Doug Schelhaas (standing) and Vern Schoolmeester and Bob Westenberg listen to Coach Rich Olson.

him sit for several minutes before sending him back into the fray. Edgerton fell behind by nine points in the first period and after rallying to within three at intermission never completely recovered to end a 21 and 1 season.

Like Kooiman, Stoel has gloomy memories of the loss in which he said only Schoolmeester played up to his ability. Stoel glumly recalled the three-for-seventeen nightmare in which his little turnaround jump shot too often rattled around the rim and spun out.

"We knew that we had a better team, but I think we might have been looking ahead a little to playing Wells, which was considered the region's powerhouse," he said. "I'll never forget three-for-seventeen . . . the ball just wouldn't fall. But St. James had a 6-foot-6 center named [Brad] Offendahl, who was a very good post man. I might have been a little intimidated having to shoot over him all night."

In the locker room afterward about the only sound for a lengthy period was Olson bouncing a silver dollar off the wall. The bus ride home was long and silent with the players somberly pondering what could have been. In addition to being one of only four teams to finish the regular season undefeated and winning the District 8 championship, the Dutchmen had the distinction of beating archrival Luverne twice, the latter being the only team to beat eventual state champion Marshall, 25 and 1.

Whatever thoughts the Edgerton underclassmen had about the next season—and the Dutchmen did have Vernon Schoolmeester, Kooiman, Curt Vanderstoop, and Boysen coming back—they didn't realize that they would be moving forward without their coach. In the June 13 edition of the *Edgerton Enterprise*, Olson's resignation was announced. The man with a four-year record of 85 and 9, three district championships and two state tournament trips had accepted a teaching and coaching job in Virginia in the backyard of his former Mountain Iron home. Olson said the decision was difficult—"I felt that I'd left behind a very good team"—and while his players understood, they were disappointed to lose the coach they had admired and respected since junior high.

"Richie was very fiery, and if you were an opposing player or fan you wouldn't like him very much," School-meester said, "but as a player and competitor in his system, I loved him all the way through. He had some gifted athletes, which was a good starting point, but to get all those people to work together was important, and Richie did that very well.

"His approach was not complex . . . nothing fancy, but it was easy to buy into."

In Virginia, Olson coached another twelve basketball seasons. He took an undefeated team to state in 1965, losing in a controversial 60 to 55 decision against Faribault, and compiled a two-school career record of 241 and 85 with five district, three region, and one state championship before stepping away to become a full-time athletic director in 1975.

As for Edgerton, the town would enjoy no more district or regional championships through the Minnesota's final years of one-divisional play, but coached by Arlen Patrick they finished 17 and 3 the following season. High school All-American and future South Dakota State great Vernon Schoolmeester ended his Edgerton career with 1,211 points, and the Dutchmen ran their string of consecutive winning seasons to eight before finishing 7 and 12 in 1967.

From 1959 through 1969, Edgerton's Public School compiled a 187 and 68 record despite sharing the town's talent pool with the Christian School. In the same period, the Christian School's record was 163 and 64.

The new coach Arlen Patrick huddles with 1963-1964 players (left) Jake Kooiman, Gary Loenhorst, Vern Schoolmeeser, Gene Boysen, and Curt Vanderstoop.

Bruce Timmer was correct, Edgerton had a great deal of basketball talent scattered in the area.

While it would be purely speculation, it could be said that the legendary 1960 Edgerton state champions established a new bench mark for not only the community, but for Region II and Region III schools in southern and southwestern Minnesota. Until 1960, the area's only championship was produced by Mountain Lake in 1939, but after the Edgerton triumph, Marshall (Region III) won in 1963, Luverne (Region II) in 1964, and Sherburn (Region II) in 1970, the final year of one-divisional competition.

Ray Merry, coach of Luverne's 1964 state championship team, was in Goodhue the year Edgerton soared to the summit in Minnesota high school basketball. He was perhaps as surprised as anyone to see the Flying Dutchmen win, but he knew enough to realize their championship run was no fluke. Harry Franz, the former Luverne coach who helped Ken Kielty organize Edgerton's junior basketball program, afforded Merry insight.

"I coached at Magnolia for a couple years in the mid-fifties after coming back from Korea, and I got to know

Harry," Merry said. "He was gracious enough to invite some of our young players over to play in Luverne. At one point, he told me, 'Keep an eye on Edgerton; they have some very good athletes coming along.' Harry had one of the best basketball minds around. In fact, I had him scout for me when I coached at Luverne.

"He started a program at the grade-school level and he didn't miss a kid. We had some exceptional players on our team in 1964."

Merry agrees that 1960 Flying Dutchmen did more than validate Franz's credibility. They delivered a salient message to small-town players and coaches not only in southwest Minnesota, but also throughout the state. The team representing the second largest high school in the smallest town ever to produce a state high school basketball champion proved that no dream is too big and no town is too small to have exceptional athletes.

The sign speaks volumes for Edgerton basketball history.

Where Are They Now?

Bill Fure spent nearly thirty five years in the education field after graduating from Luther College in Iowa, and one of his favorite stops—certainly his most memorable—was his tenure as superintendent at Edgerton High School.

"I lived a charmed life in Edgerton," he said of the Dutch community in southwest Minnesota. "I was always impressed with the quality of the school staff, and, of all the schools I was in, the Edgerton kids were probably the best bunch. There were a lot of excellent students and few distractions."

Of particular note was the high school's 1960 state championship, an achievement in which their amazing feat reflected not only their basketball prowess but their character on and off the court. That each Flying Dutchman on that team achieved more than a modicum of success comes as no surprise to the veteran administrator whose career included stops in six schools, the last one being Sauk Rapids, where he served twelve years before retiring in 1984.

"No one is perfect, but as a group they were exceptional," Fure said. "Their response to authority and direction was more than you could have expected. And for being so young they handled success well . . . they were excellent role models."

Fure said the players had a strong support system in school, from Coach Rich Olson and his assistant the late John Rath to teachers such as longtime faculty member Charles Deremo, a no-nonsense teacher who insisted that not one of the Flying Dutchmen players gave him a moment of grief. The community also provided positive support, always encouraging but never indulging, but the major source of their bedrock character came from their homes. No one was from affluence—most were farm kids who understood a hard day's work—but all were endowed with rich family tradition that kept them well grounded on and off the court. All but one had both parents to guide them; Darrell Kreun's mother, Johanna, tirelessly managed to support and guide four children after her husband's death when Darrell was a toddler.

All the virtues that made them successful student-athletes helped earn them more than a small measure of success beyond high school. Most of them graduated from college, with the majority becoming teacher-coaches or working in social service, while those who immediately stepped into the working world fared extremely well.

Each conceded that the achievement had a profound impact on his life, but none dwelled on his contributions. They scattered throughout the state and nation, and lost touch with some of their former teammates, but throughout their adult lives they have continued to think as a team, perhaps the most endearing factor in the state's boundless memory of a special team in a special era.

DARYL STEVENS

AFTER GRADUATING FROM HIGH SCHOOL, Daryl played football, basketball, and track and field at Worthington Junior College. He finished his collegiate years at St. Cloud State University where he played basketball for Red Severson.

Daryl and Pam Stevens.

Daryl graduated in 1967 and began his career at Anoka State Hospital, working as a rehabilitation therapist. In 1973 he transferred to the Minnesota Corrections Facility in St. Cloud where he was employed as a chemical dependency assessor and caseworker until his retirement in 2005. Daryl and his wife Pam enjoy running, biking, and swimming, and compete in duathlons (run, bike, run) and tristhlons (swim, bike, run).

In September 2007 they completed the Ironman Wisconsin (2.4-mile swim, 112-mile bike, 26.2-mile run). They also planned on racing in the Hawaiian Ironman in October 2008.

Daryl and Pam have been race directors of the Apple Duathlon in Sartell, Minnesota, for twenty-six years. Daryl has two daughters, Leah and Jessica.

"I didn't notice until many years later how much of an impact the little town of Edgerton had on the state's history, and the pride that it has instilled in me."

DEAN VERDOES

DEAN GRADUATED FROM MACALESTER College in 1964 with a bachelor of arts in mathematics. From 1964 to 1969 he taught mathematics and coached basketball in Clarkfield, Minnesota. He held a similar position at Madison in 1969-1970 and then at, Woodbury Junior High School during 1970-1971.

In 1972 he received his master's degree in education administration from the University of St. Thomas in St. Paul, Minnesota, and in 1975 completed his education administration certification at St. Thomas.

Dean and Barb Verdoes.

Dean's career took him to Henry Sibley High School in Mendota Heights, Minnesota, in 1971, where he remained for the next twenty-eight years. In addition to teaching mathematics, he coached basketball, soccer, and golf until 1986. From then until his retirement in 1999, Dean served as the athletic director and assistant principal at Henry Sibley.

He was a member of the Minnesota State High School League Board for four years and the Region 3AA committee for six years. He was chairman of the latter for four years. Although retired, Dean has helped administer many state tournaments.

He also is an avid golfer, and enjoys fishing, and hunting.

Dean married Barb Palm in 1969, and today they like to travel around the United States.

"One of the positive results of winning the tournament was being recruited to play basketball at Macalester College in St. Paul, Minnesota. Macalester turned out to be the perfect place for me to go to college. I had the opportunity to receive a great education and also to play basketball for four years. I also met many wonderful students and teachers and developed many lifelong friendships".

"Because of my positive experiences with both high school and college basketball, I decided to become a high school math teacher and coach. It was a rewarding occupation and I coached basketball for over twenty years. In reflecting over the past many years, one of the really nice things that happened to me was the opportunity to meet many basketball fans that were interested in knowing about the Edgerton team. It always amazes me that people are able to remember details about something that happened nearly fifty years ago."

BOB WIARDA

Bob Wiarda.

AFTER GRADUATING FROM HIGH SCHOOL, Bob attended Morningside College in Sioux City, Iowa, on a baseball scholarship. In an outstanding baseball career at Morningside, one game in particular sticks out: The game in which he pitched and won 2 to 1 over defending champion Iowa State.

Bob married his high school sweetheart, Toni Maas, while still in college, and they have two children, Mark and Heidi Allison.

Bob began his career at the corrections facility at Willow River, Minnesota, in 1964, where he was a senior corrections officer until 1980. Bob then transferred to the St. Cloud Reformatory and worked in minimum security until 1986. At that time, he took a job in Duluth at Woodland Hills, a rehabilitation center for Minnesota workers.

Bob retired after 2000 and lives in Duluth, where he enjoys fishing the St. Louis River with Mark.

"One of the things that has endured is the pleasant memories of being the underdogs and always believing in ourselves as a team. I still enjoy when meeting people and they discover my Edgerton roots, and can still name the starting five on the 1960 team."

LEROY GRAPHENTEEN

Soon after graduation, LeRoy began working for Central Telephone Company, where he held several managerial positions. He retired in 1996 as regional business accounts manager in Burnsville, Minnesota.

After retiring, LeRoy and his wife, the former Patty Johnson of Pipestone,

LeRoy and Patty Graphenteen.

moved back to Fairmont, Minnesota. He now works part time in a local hardware store.

LeRoy and Patty have three children and ten grandchildren, whom they enjoy watching participate in sports and school activities. They also enjoy fishing and shopping for antiques.

"While winning the 1960 State title was a very important moment in my life, the remarkable friendships, the irrepressible teamwork and the extraordinary support from family, friends, and community were what significantly impacted my life. Every player, manager, coach, and fan exhibited unlimited pride and enormous character. By playing for Edgerton, I acquired a great sense of enthusiasm, discipline and confidence that has helped me become successful in all aspects of my life."

DARRELL KREUN

IN AUGUST, 1961 DARRELL enrolled in Northwestern College at Orange City, Iowa, from which he graduated in 1965, with a degree in education. He earned numerous awards: four-year letterman in basketball and baseball, All-Conference two years in basketball and baseball, and was Northwestern Athlete of the Year in 1964. Darrell was inducted as a charter member into Northwestern's Athletics Hall of Fame in 1986.

Darrell and Judy Kreun.

EDGERTON

His first teaching and coaching basketball position was in Hanska, Minnesota, from 1965 to 1968. From there, he went to Gaylord in 1968, where he held the head basketball position until 1990 when the school was consolidated with Arlington-Green Isle. He continued as head basketball coach at Sibley East until his retirement in 2000. As coach at Gaylord and Sibley East, Darrell recorded fifteen conference titles, three regional titles, and was a state tournament participant in 1969, 1972, and finished third in 1999. In thirty-four years of coaching he compiled a record of 587 wins and 216 losses and was one of the top five winning coaches in Minnesota. Darrell was inducted into the Minnesota Basketball Coaches Association "Hall of Fame in 1999.

Darrell married his girlfriend from high school, Judy Roelofs, and they have three children, Kelli, Tadd, and Traci, and four grandchildren. Darrell and Judy moved to northern Minnesota, near Marcell, after retirement.

"Bringing pride and recognition to the community and putting Edgerton on the map. Almost fifty years later many people can remember the starting five and the teams accomplishments. The success helped me gain scholarships and achieve a degree. To reminiscence each year at state tournament is special.

Finally it showed me what a small school with dedicated athletes and coaches can accomplish with teamwork, hard work, and the desire to succeed against all odds in a sport we dearly loved."

DEAN VEENHOF

AFTER GRADUATION DEAN attended Bradley University on a basketball scholarship. After one semester he realized he was in over his head and transferred to Augustana College in Sioux Falls, South Dakota, where he played basketball for two years. However, his education was interrupted when he was drafted into the United States Army. He served in Vietnam for fifteen months.

Judy and Dean Veenhof.

After his discharge in May of 1967, Dean went to New York where he proposed to Augustana College sweetheart Judy, who now was teaching on her native Staten Island. They married in December 1967 and settled in Fridley, Minnesota. Dean, through the G.I. Bill, and Judy's help, received his bachelor's degree in December 1969 from Huron College. In 1970 the couple moved to New York, just as Dean promised Judy they would. Dean's career as a physical education teacher spanned twenty-eight years in New York, three in Edmeston, one in Cooperstown, and twenty-four in Gibertsville. He also taught driver education, and coached basketball and other sports. Dean was involved in the State Athletic Association and served as president of Section IV from 1990 to 1994.

From 1998 to 2001 Dean was president of New York State Public High School Athletic Association and continues to be involved as a past president.

Church is equally important and Judy and Dean are active members of the First Presbyterian Church in Gilbertsville.

Judy and Dean have three daughters, Mieke, Meghan, and Kristi, who were all excellent athletes in high school.

Dean now drives tour buses, and for nine years in the summer has driven the team bus for the Oneonta Tigers. Eight players who began their careers in Oneonta are now playing for Detroit.

NORM MUILENBURG

Norm earned his pharmacy degree in 1966 from South Dakota State University, then joined the Peace Corps and spent two years in Ethiopia. He met his future wife, Marjorie, while in Peace Corps training. After returning to the United States, they lived in the Twin Cities for four years before moving to Portland, Oregon, in 1973.

Norm works for HMO Kaiser Permanente. Norm and Marjorie have two grown sons, Andy and Pete, and two grandchildren, Brady and Lucy. Marge retired, but Norm is still working full-time for Kaiser in Portland.

Marjorie and Norm Muilenburg.

"I really felt more like an observer than a participant, since I played so little. Nevertheless, it provided memories and thrills to last a lifetime. The most amazing thing to me is that when people ask where I'm from and hear 'Edgerton, Minnesota,' it seems like that town and that basketball team is known the world over. And it is just astounding that so many people can list at least four of the starting five from that team. We truly lived the movie *Hoosiers*."

JIM ROOS

IN THE FALL OF 1961, Jim enrolled at Concordia in St. Paul, a two-year college where he played basketball. In 1963, he transferred to Mankato State and was a member of the 1963-1964 basketball team. He followed that with a two-year education stop at Concordia in Fort Wayne where he played basketball for one year. In 1966 Jim began ministry studies at Concordia Lutheran Seminary in St. Louis, Missouri. He also played basketball at the seminary, and the 1967-1968 "Preachers" won the Concordia Invitational basketball tournament. Jim was named most valuable player.

Jim and Judy Roos.

After graduating from the seminary in 1970, Jim started Neighborhood Enterprises, a housing business/ministry that provides rental housing for about 200 lower-income families. Since 2005 he also has led the fight against eminent-domain abuse in Missouri.

Jim met Judy in 1966 when she was a nursing student in St. Louis. Jim dated her almost two years before they decided on a double wedding in Wisconsin Dells, Judy's home. In 1968 Judy and Jim were married along with her sister and her groom. Jim and Judy have two sons, Matt and Tim.

Jim enjoys swimming and biking, and for the last three summers he has biked 450 miles across Iowa in the RABRAI seven-day rides. Jim, being a workaholic, feels that the bike rides restore some balance between work and rest.

TOM WARREN

After high school, Tom attended Iowa State for one year before transferring to Dakota State University in Madison, South Dakota. He graduated in 1966 with a degree in mathematics and physical science. Tom then attended graduate school at the University of South Dakota in Vermillion and graduated with a master's degree in mathematics and science.

Tom spent thirty-three years teaching math

Tom and Cheryl Warren.

and science: eight years in Jasper, ten years in Albany, and fifteen years in Alexandria. He coached seventh- and eighth-grade basketball for five years in Jasper (three undefeated seasons).

Tom married Cheryl Kearin, an elementary teacher from Madison, South Dakota, in August of 1966. They have two children, Jeff and Gina, and two grandchildren.

Tom was a Scout leader, and his hobbies are golfing, hunting, and wood carving. Tom and Cheryl also have enjoyed a number of trips abroad.

"It gave me an opportunity to meet players from the other teams in the tournament and discuss the games. We also discussed what had happened during their lives. I think that winning the tournament has helped me meet and converse with people. It also helped me to coach winning basketball teams for the ten years I coached."

ROB DYKSTRA

Rob Dykstra.

Rob Dykstra was a sophomore reserve forward on the 1960 Edgerton championship team and started his final two seasons, including 1961 when the Dutchmen returned to the state tournament. He graduated from Edgerton in 1962 and worked locally until making enough money to attend the Spartan School of Aeronautics in

Tulsa, Oklahoma, where he was trained to become a commercial pilot and flight instructor.

He joined the South Dakota Air National Guard in 1964 and was assigned as a jet engine mechanic on a fighter aircraft. While in basic training, he played basketball for the Amarillo Air Force Base in Texas.

He moved to Redwood Falls, Minnesota, where he managed the airport, gave flight instruction, and piloted charter flights. After two years, he became a full-time technician in the Air National Guard and remained a member for thirty-nine years, attaining the rank of command chief master sergeant of the 114th Fighter Wing.

He retired in 2003, but since flying remained his passion and he became manager of the Pipestone Municipal Airport in Pipestone, Minnesota, and is owner and operator of Country Aire, LLC, which provides flight training for all levels from student pilots to airline transport pilots. He has logged more than 12,000 accident-free hours and is an authorized federal aviation inspector.

Rob married Dianne Mathers of Pipestone, and they live in Sioux Falls. Diane and Rob have two children, Todd and Dawn, and seven grandchildren.

"When we won the state title it was great, but what I didn't realize at the time was the work, discipline, and training it takes to be a winner. What Rich Olson gave me and others was a "can do" attitude. When I went to basic training, I tried out for the base team, figuring that I would be a substitute, but I started. In Sioux Falls, I coached YMCA basketball from grades four through twelve, and our sixth-grade team won the Tri-State YMCA Championship. Perhaps I emulated Ole, and for that I say, "Thanks," for him and the Edgerton experience."

DARWIN D.J. FEY

Number 22, graduated in 1962, was married and raised three children, and has three grandchildren.

D.J. started an advertising specialty company, invested in rental real estate, and is part owner of a commercial carpet company. He retired in 1996 at the age of fifty-two.

D.J. Fey.

D.J. who remarried after a storybook romance in Jamaica, now lives in Arizona. He loves to play golf and has a low round of 69. He still gets asked about the Cinderella basketball team from Edgerton, Minnesota.

"If you have a dream, a great desire and an undying belief that you can accomplish something, when you put all your efforts in that direction, you may find that your dreams as well as many other desires will come true."

LARRY SCHOOLMEESTER

Larry enlisted in the Air Force in 1965 and was sent to Lackland Air Force Base in San Antonio, Texas. After graduating from IBM School in Wichita Falls, Texas he was promoted to sergeant. He was discharged in 1968.

After working in Sioux Falls for a short time, Larry returned home in 1970 and was employed at the Edgerton

Farmers Co-op until his retirement in 2004.

Larry's wife, Marilyn, who teaches at Edgerton Public School, live in Edgerton. They have two sons Tim and Tom and a daughter Julie. They like spending time with their two grandchildren, and Larry enjoys hunting and fishing.

Marilyn and Larry Schoolmeester.

"Being part of the team that won the Minnesota state championship was the highlight of my high school years. It is always surprising that wherever we travel, we meet someone who asks us about the 1960 state tournament—'The Minnesota Hoosiers' story!"

DOUG VANDER BEEK

AFTER GRADUATION FROM HIGH SCHOOL, Doug attended Dunwoody Institute and graduated with an associate degree in architectural drafting. He went to work at Lampert Lumber in 1962, but was drafted into the military and served in 1964 and 1965.

Doug married Maryann Mesman in 1966. They lived in the Twin Cities where Doug worked for Lampert Lumber until 1980. At that time they moved to Edgerton and Doug, along with Lee Tinklenberg, established a lumberyard.

In 1994 Doug and Maryann moved to Sioux Falls, South Dakota, where Doug managed Scott Lumber until

Doug and Maryann Vander Beek

2006. He partially retired, but continued for a while to work part time for Scott as a lumber buyer.

Doug and Maryann have three children, Steve, Jill, and Craig, and four grandchildren.

They enjoy spending time with their children and grandchildren, a pleasure made easy since they all live within sixty miles of each other.

Now that both are retired, Doug and Maryann split their time between Sioux Falls and Chandler, Arizona, their winter home.

"I still think of that wonderful year and the experience of winning the state title. I don't think many of us fully realized what an accomplishment this was at the time of the tournament. It took me time to realize the significance of this accomplishment. I have been able to apply many of the lessons we learned that year to my life. I was not a player, but I worked closely with the team. The lessons that were important to me and that I have applied to my life and to my career are those of teamwork, dedication, fortitude and a commitment to a common goal."

SOURCES

The *Edgerton Enterprise* and columns by former sports columnist Arlie Steen.

The *Worthington Globe* and columns by the paper's sports editor, the late Corky Brace.

The *Mountain Lake Observer*.

Mesabi Daily News.

Edgerton Minnesota, A History 1879-1979, by Sandra Beckering.

Column notes and comments from John Egan, former *Sioux Falls Argus-Leader*.

Gopher State Greatness by Joel B. Krenz.

The late Charles Deremo's handwritten accounts of Edgerton High history.

Northern Graphics and Video Production, Dan Truebenbach and Tadd Kreun.

The Minnesota Historical Society collection of *Minneapolis Star-Tribune*, *St. Paul Pioneer Press*, and *Luverne's Rock County Herald*. Attribution was given on all quotes acquired from one of the newspaper's exclusive stories.

EDGERTON

The Minnesota Historical Society is an incredible source for anyone writing a book, conducting genealogy or doing any type of family or community research.

Edgerton High School yearbooks from the late 1940s through the early 1960s.

The South Dakota State University sports information office for photos involving former SDSU athletes.

The Macalester College sports information office.

The University of Minnesota sports information office.

Bill Swank, southern California author and sports historian.

Calla R. Scott, *The History of Edgerton, Minnesota.*

1960 Minnesota State High School League Basketball Program.

INDEX

Ackerman, Jerry, 97.
Adrian, 17, 52, 78, 79, 84, 90, 186, 190.
Albert Lea, 37, 39, 48, 108.
Alevizos, Roger, 130.
Allaman, Dennis, 187.
Amboy, 70, 108.
Anderson, Chet, 194.
Anderson, Harold, 162.
Anderson, Keith, 132.
Archer, Ron, 98, 99.
Arlich, Don, 131.
Argyle, 93, 133.
Ashbough, Alfred, 5, 6.
Ashbough, Virgil, 5, 6.
Atwater, 96, 197.
Austin, ix, xii, 7, 15, 99, 107, 108, 117, 128, 129, 131-134, 137, 138, 142, 144, 146, 152, 155, 157-163, 189.

Baar, Daryl, 184.
Bacon, Dorthy, 10.
Baker, Bob, 186.

Baker, Jim, 18.
Baldwin, Clay, 8.
Baldwin, Fred, 27, 28, 121.
Barton, Doug, 130, 147.
Beaver Creek, 16, 20, 28, 32, 36, 57, 87, 91, 95, 188, 189, 192, 204.
Beckering, Datus, 17.
Beckering, Roland, 29.
Beckering, Sandra, 4, 227.
Belluzzo, O.J. "Ner", 129, 130.
Belview, 50.
Bemidji, 50, 107, 133, 189, 195, 196, 198, 199.
Berger, Dave, 194.
Berven, Ove, 128, 129, 133, 134, 157, 159-161.
Beukelman, Jan, 46.
Beukelman, John, 27.
Black, Tom, 103.
Bloomington, 59, 61, 131, 165, 166, 185, 187.
Blue Earth, 7.
Boelman, Junior, 95.

229

Bolluyt, Arnold, 19.
Bolstorff, Doug, 61.
Booher, Bill, 134.
Bostic, Sid, 95, 96, 98-103.
Bouma, Adrian, 170.
Bouma, John, 18.
Boysen, Gene, 203, 204, 206, 208.
Brace, Corky, 90, 98, 106, 152, 227.
Brancich, Jasper, 129, 130, 140, 141.
Brands, John, 33, 34.
Brewster, 17.
Brink, Leslie, 20.
Brockberg, Dean, 37.
Brod, Nick, 103.
Broekhuis, Donley, 37.
Broekhuis, Helen, 11.
Broekhuis, Lois, 11.
Brooks, Billy, 20.
Brooks, Milo, 8.
Brooks, Ruth, 11.
Brouwer, Joe, 48, 49.
Brouwer, John, 33.
Brovold, James H., 11-15, 17-20, 22, 23, 26, 27, 51, 61, 121.
Brower, Alma, 10.
Brown, Terry, 134, 158.
Bruggers, Bob, 106.
Buhl, 185.
Bulger, Don, 133, 134, 157.
Butler, Earl, 134.
Bylsma, John, 34, 36.
Bystedt, Gary, 130.

Campbell, Paul, 135.
Canby, 95.
Carlton, 128, 131, 132.
Carrington, Jim, 195.
Ceylon, 193.
Chandler, 85, 88, 89, 94, 96, 97, 185, 192, 200, 205.

Chatfield, 49, 59, 117.
Chisholm, xii, 92, 122, 123, 127, 129, 130, 137, 139, 140, 141, 143, 144, 146, 147, 156, 163.
Christians, John, 20.
Clark, Eddie, 203.
Cloquet, 93, 106.
Coleraine, 129.
Colwell, Gary, 95.
Conley, Jerrol, 87.
Cook, 65.
Cooney, Jed, 36.
Courtney, C. Wayne, 40, 43, 46, 188, 189, 196, 197.
Cragoe, Jim, 58, 71.
Cronk, Ray, 50.
Crosby-Ironton, 132.

Danube, 106, 195.
Dassel, 26, 32, 33.
Davis, Bill, 130, 131, 133, 141, 142, 144, 147-151, 154, 156, 162, 163.
Dehner, William, 10, 11.
De Boer, John, 169.
DeGroot, Melvin, 49, 51, 52.
DeJong, Casey, v, 23-29, 42.
DeJong, Geraldine, 11.
DeJong, Roland, 19.
De Koekkoek, Lewella, 11.
Dell Rapids, 36.
Delaney, Ray, 5, 6.
De La Salle, 196.
De Mots, Bill, 11.
Den Ouden, Arlo, 146.
Den Ouden, Nys, 152.
Den Ouden, Tom, 54.
Den Cote, Bob, 37.
Dethmers, Russell, 18.
Detroit Lakes, 132.
DeWitt, Bernard, 51.

EDGERTON

Dick, Charlie, 111, 115.
Dodge Center, 93, 106, 133, 135.
Draheim, Charles, 134.
Dropp, Bob, 129, 130, 141.
Duluth Morgan Park, 108, 124, 195.
Duluth Central, 93, 106, 189, 195, 199.
Dykstra, Bob, 21, 82, 83, 182, 183, 186-188, 191, 200, 201, 222.

Edgerton, Emma, 166.
Eernisse, Harvey, 51, 52, 54, 57, 72.
Egan, John, xiv, 90, 188, 227.
Ellgen, Walter "Spike," 11, 16.
Ellsworth, 48, 50, 53, 54, 57, 58, 70, 71, 84, 85, 87, 88, 90, 95, 103, 171, 172, 187.
Elson, David, 33.
Embury, Steve, 133.
Eng, Marie, 10.
Enger, Ollie, 46.
Enroth, Dick, 135.
Epp, Henry, 115.
Epp, Ruben, 65, 115.
Erdman, Bob, viii, 53, 92, 190, 193.
Esko, 93, 106.
Espeland, Leonard, 132.

Faribault, 7, 207.
Fairmont, 193, 216.
Farrell, Gene, 154.
Fawbush, Lee, 199.
Fey, Darwin, 82, 186, 200, 224.
Fey, D.J., 21, 201.
Fey, Leon, 184, 203.
Fey, Norman, 46, 51, 52, 54, 82, 83, 90.
Flandreau, South Dakota, 30, 31, 35.

Ford, Eldon "Docky," 13, 19.
Forest Lake, 93, 96, 106.
Fortier, Bun, 195, 198.
Fosston, 7.
Fransen, John, 32-35, 79, 203.
Franz, Harry, 46, 208, 209.
Fulda, 20, 58, 94, 96.
Fure, Bill, v, 49, 58-61, 69, 73, 92, 107, 117, 120, 143, 155, 169, 171, 172, 176, 210, 211.

Garmaker, Dick, 43.
Gertz, Bea, 10.
Gettler, Dennis, 111.
Gibson, Charles H., 48.
Gilbert, 62, 64, 122, 159.
Gilman, Mona, 145.
Gjerde, Mark, 130.
Glasrud, Bob, 98, 99, 103.
Glasrud, Dave, 98, 99.
Goehle, Hugo, 89, 98, 171, 190, 192.
Golberg, Dick, 134.
Grand Meadow, 10.
Grand Rapids, 7.
Granite Falls, 127, 132, 137, 138, 144, 146, 156, 162.
Grantz, Dick, 111.
Graphenteen, Arnie, 27, 29-31, 33, 80.
Graphenteen, Clarence, 13, 23, 24, 80.
Graphenteen, Les, 32, 36, 37, 80.
Graphenteen, LeRoy, x, xiii, 21, 45, 46, 49, 51, 52, 72, 73, 80, 82, 83, 88, 90, 92, 110, 141, 148, 150-153, 157-163, 168, 174, 178, 179, 182, 186, 191, 200, 215.
Griffin, Margie, 145.
Groen, Glen, 46.
Gruys, Dean, 28-32.

231

EDGERTON

Gruys, Peter, 28-30.
Gulbrandson, Harry, 11.
Gutzke, Don, 33.

Hagen, Jon, 50.
Hagemann, Andy, 50, 51, 92, 190, 192, 196.
Halstad, 65, 195.
Hanamann, H.J., 122.
Hankins, Ivan Dale, 23, 24.
Hannan, Dave, 129.
Hansen, Larry, 131, 138, 162.
Hansen, Ron, 95.
Hardwick, 16, 83, 122.
Hart, Doug, 99.
Hart, Len, 98.
Hartman, Sid, 112, 166, 178.
Hawley, 96, 97.
Hayden, Dick, 25-34.
Hegna, Gerald, 132, 138, 162.
Hemingson, Lyle, 132, 138.
Hendricks, Norm, 37.
Hibbing, 63.
Higgins, Larry, 199.
Hills, 16, 17, 30, 54, 84, 89, 94-98, 171, 181, 187, 188, 192.
Hoffman, Chuck, 29, 30.
Howard Lake, 26, 33, 34.
Hoyme, N.B., 20.
Huisken, George, 37, 49.
Huisken, Joe, 13.
Hull, 30.
Hulstein, Eddie, 33.
Huska, John, 129.

Jacobs, Rose Marie, 11.
Jacobs, Wayne, 18.
Jacobson, Lance, 134.
Jasper, xiii, 10, 15, 20, 23, 32, 36, 50, 52, 55, 58, 71, 72, 80, 82, 84, 85, 87, 90, 96, 105, 107, 129,

171, 185, 188, 202, 204, 222.
Jelgerhuis, Elmer, 20.
Johlfs, Art, 189.
Johnson, Bruce, 98, 99.
Johnson, Dennis, 130, 131, 154.
Johnson, Mert, 95.
Johnson, Ron, 50.
Jolink, Margaret, 10.
Jones, Donald, 19.

Kekke, Ken, 129.
Kennedy, 107.
Kielty, Ken, vii, xiii, 37-50, 52-56, 58-60, 72-74, 80, 114, 208.
Kindt, Ron, 46.
Kingsley, Kenneth, 5, 6, 8, 9.
Klindt, Arnold, 18, 19.
Kline, Lyle, 134.
Klotzbach, Ed, 129.
Klumper, Andrew, 33.
Klumper, Henry, 33.
Kok, G.S., 146.
Kooiman, Bertus, 174.
Kooiman, Elmer, 43, 44, 47, 75, 76, 168.
Kooiman, Jake, 47, 183, 203-206, 208.
Kooiman, Kathryn, 11.
Kooiman, Pat, 43, 156.
Kooiman, Thelma, 43, 44.
Koster, Ken, 186.
Koster, Sid, 27.
Krenz, Joel B., xiv.
Kreun, Carroll, 34.
Kreun, Darrell, x, xi, xiii, 21, 45, 46, 49, 51, 52, 54, 70, 72, 76, 80-84, 86-90, 93, 97, 100, 101, 103-105, 110, 114, 115, 118, 122, 123, 126, 138, 140, 146, 149-151, 153, 158, 159, 161, 162, 169, 174, 176, 181-183, 186, 191, 192, 194, 198-200,

210, 216.
Kreun, Duane, 33, 34, 36, 153.
Kreun, Johanna, 210.
Kreun, Judy Roelofs, xi.
Kreun, Mavis, 145, 170.
Kreun, Ron, 81, 152.
Krohn, John, 111.
Krosschell, Don, 18.
Krosschell, Marv, 19.
Kruger, Bill, 134.
Kundla, John, 157.
Kunze, Terry, 198.

Lakefield, 96.
Lake Wilson, 49, 50, 53, 84, 88, 187.
Landhuis, Duane, 37, 48.
Lary, George, 130.
Lee, Roy, 172.
Lenderts, Duke, 95.
Lensink, Everett, 23-25.
Leota, 171, 183.
Lester, 32.
Loenhorst, Gary, 203, 208.
Lorenzen, Melvin, 34.
Lorenzen, Peter, 20.
Lucas, Tom, 23, 24.
Lundeen, Ralph, 69.
Luverne, vii, viii, 7, 10, 14-19, 32,
    35, 36, 46, 47, 49-51, 53, 58, 68,
    72, 78, 89, 91-98, 100, 104, 106,
    112, 122, 127, 128, 171, 176, 182,
    185, 189, 190-193, 196, 202, 204,
    206, 208, 209.
Lutz, Mac, 130, 131, 148, 163.
Lynd, 15, 117, 128, 156.

Madison, South Dakota, 7, 213,
    221, 222.
Maetzold, Butsie, 133.
Magnolia, 17, 28, 32, 84-86, 89, 94-
    97, 171, 172, 188, 189, 202, 208.

Mankato, 7, 15, 29, 41, 42, 51, 79,
    106-110, 112, 113, 128, 135,
    138, 139, 143, 156, 163, 194,
    204.
Mapleton, viii, 108.
Markl, B., 203.
Marshall, 95, 96, 98, 101, 143,
    172, 206, 208.
Mattson, George, 172.
McArthur, Jim, 105.
McKay, George, 50.
McLaughlin, Jim, 167.
McLenighan, Harry, 130.
McVenes, Dennis, 28-30.
Meacham, Fletcher, 5, 6.
Meacham, Harris, 12.
Meacham, Lawrence, 5, 6.
Mechanic Arts, 8, 131.
Melrose, 93, 132, 137, 138, 144,
    156, 162.
Mencel, Chuck, 43.
Menning, Merlin, 46.
Merry, Ray, 208, 209.
Millis, Orson, 13.
Minneota, 86.
Mohr, Bill, 92.
Monat, Bill, 65-68, 108.
Montevideo, 144.
Moorhead, 176, 185.
Mountain Iron, 63-66, 70, 73, 207.
Mountain Lake, 7, 15, 46, 65, 72,
    74, 79, 106, 111-116, 138, 143,
    163, 193, 208.
Moss, Toni, 119.
Muilenburg, Alvin, 19.
Muilenburg, Norm, 21, 82, 83,
    186, 188, 219.

Naismith, Dr. James, 1-4.
Nelson, Marsh, 121.
Nettleton, Curt, 115.

EDGERTON

Nettleton, Mack, 11, 114, 115.
New Praque, 50.
New Ulm, 172.
Nickerson, Ernest O., 9-11, 13, 14, 18, 22, 23.
Nielson, Dick, 132.
Norgard, Hal, 131, 142.
North St. Paul, 124, 131, 142-144, 156, 162.
Northfield, 7, 12.
Novoselac, Ron, 129, 141.

Offendahl, Brad, 206.
Olson, Alice, 64.
Olson, Bob, 65.
Olson, Floyd "Govie," 63, 65.
Olson, Marlys [Hannay], v, 69, 116, 121, 176.
Olson, Ragnar, 64.
Olson, Ralph, 64.
Olson, Rich, v, viii, ix, xiv, 48, 59-74, 76, 77, 80-83, 86-88, 92, 94, 97, 98, 100, 101, 105, 108, 112, 113, 115, 116, 119-123, 125, 128, 129, 135, 136, 138, 141-143, 149, 151-155, 157, 158, 160, 161, 166, 167, 172, 174, 175, 177-180, 182-184, 186, 190. 194-196, 198-203, 205-207, 211, 223.
Okabena, 17, 193.
Oliver, Raymond, 19, 20.
Ortonville, 132.
Ostendorf, Marvin, 138.
Otto, Ed, 98-100, 102, 103.
Owatonna, 176.

Page, Mitchell, 134.
Pals, Curt, 184.
Patrick, Arlen, 206, 208.
Patrick Henry, 193.
Patterson, Mike, 198.

Pearson, Bob, 133.
Pemberton, 15, 107, 108, 205.
Peterson, Cliff, 9, 121.
Peterson, Ted, 90, 179, 180, 185.
Phelps, Jack, 198.
Pipestone, 2, 4, 15-17, 21, 24, 25, 28, 30-32, 35, 36, 42, 46, 50, 52, 60, 70, 74, 79, 92, 94-96, 98-102, 104, 108, 112, 113, 122, 125, 127, 135, 138, 143, 163, 172, 176, 178, 202, 205, 215, 223.
Plainview, 7.
Pool, Bill, 118.
Pool, Curtis, 184, 203.
Pool, Duane, 34.
Pool, Lloyd, 37.
Pool, Owen, 29.
Pool, William, 169, 170.
Prins, Norm, 118, 183, 184, 191, 203.
Puhl, Gene, 105.

Radotich, Tom, 129.
Raque, Rick, 11.
Ramseth, George, 172.
Rapp, Larry, 50, 51, 93.
Rasmussen, Wayne, 103.
Rath, John, 51, 123, 176, 211.
Rath, Sally, 176.
Raymond, Butch, 53, 55, 71, 85.
Red Wing, 7.
Redwood Falls, 143, 172, 223.
Reed, Clayton, 133, 134, 138, 158-160, 162.
Renville, 93, 106.
Richardson, Tom, 62.
Riley, George, 110.
Rochester, 59, 98.
Roelofs, James, 12, 125.
Roelofs, Judy, xi, 216.
Roels, Harvey, 130.

234

EDGERTON

Roetman, Stanley, 17, 19.
Rolfs, Lester, 18.
Romkema, John, 20.
Roos, Jim, 21, 72, 82, 83, 91, 92, 135, 182, 186, 220.
Roos, Judy, 220.
Roosevelt, 19, 33, 34, 39, 40, 43, 46, 185, 188-191, 195-197, 200.
Roseau, 133.
Round Lake, 97.
Rupner, Ruby, 11.
Russell, 172.
Ruthton, 172, 176.
Sadek, Bob, 130, 131, 147-149, 151, 154, 155, 162.
St. Cloud Cathedral, 132.
St. James, viii, 108, 193, 194, 204-206.
St. Louis Park, 131.
St. Marie, John, 166-168.
St. Peter, 105, 107, 115.
Saum, Donald, 5, 6.
Schaap, Arvin, 184.
Schaap, Marion, 20.
Schankl, Orville, 108.
Schelhaas, Albertus, 29.
Schelhaas, Doug, 182, 186, 203-205.
Schelhaas, George, 183.
Schelhaas, Glen, 48.
Schley, David, 63, 64.
Schmeider, Jack, 134.
Schmidt, Arsene, 203.
Schmidt, Harvey, 170, 171.
Schnyder, Angie, 10.
Schnyders, Archie, 37.
Scholten, Marie, 10.
Schoolmeester, Bev, 46.
Schoolmeester, Bruce, 34, 37.
Schoolmeester, Jerold, 29.
Schoolmeester, Larry, 21, 82, 150, 182, 183, 186, 188, 200, 201,
224, 225.
Schoolmeester, Marilyn, v, 225.
Schoolmeester, Vernon "Tonto," 47, 183, 200-207.
Schulhouse, Ernest, 18.
Schultz, Howie, 131.
Schumacher, Gary, 99, 133, 134, 160, 162.
Schweim, Leroy, 108, 110, 111, 113, 194.
Scott, Calla R., 4.
Scott, Leonard, 8.
Seltz, Dick, 161.
Sherburn, 106, 110-112, 114, 208.
Siebert, Dick, 41.
Simonovich, Bill, 62.
Skarich, Brad, 129.
Slayton, 15-17, 24, 25, 29, 32, 53, 71, 91, 95, 96, 182, 185, 190, 202, 204.
Snow, Cleon, 5, 6.
Snyder, Andy, 159.
Snyder, Don, 187.
Snyder, Irma, 11.
Southwest Christian School, 21, 203.
Stahl, Don, 129.
Standly, Bill, 34-39, 42, 44, 47, 48, 108, 115.
Strassburg, Dale, 46.
Strassburg, Darrell, 18.
Steen, Arlie, 48, 49, 51, 54.
Stevens, Daryl, xiv, 21, 46, 50, 52, 82, 83, 85, 91, 110, 135, 140, 148, 150, 161, 176, 181, 211, 212.
Stevens, Duane, 37.
Stevens, Evelyn, 10.
Stevens, Larry, 186.
Stevens, Milford, 29.
Stevens, Pam, 212.

EDGERTON

Stevens, Pearl, 10.
Stillwater, 7, 167.
Stoel, Bernie, 183, 201-206.
Story, Hartley, 131.
Stuessy, Dwight, 68.
Steussy, Lloyd, 194
Szepanski, Bill, 130, 147.

Templeman, Mary, 11.
Thief River Falls, 107, 132, 133, 137, 138, 144, 160, 189.
Thorson, Larry, 37, 48.
Timmer, Bruse, 117, 118, 184, 202, 208.
Timmer, Doug, 118.
Tinklenberg, Clarence, 37, 46.
Tinklenberg, Harris, 37, 48.
Tinklenberg, Joyce, 170.
Tinklenberg, Lee, 225.
Tinklenberg, Leroy, 23, 24.
Tinklenberg, Robert, 33.
Tinklenberg, Virg, 37.
Tolsma, Florence, 10.
Totushek, John, 197.
Trichel, Blaine, 18.
Trosky, 4.
Tschetter, Henry, 105.

Van Bockel, John, 20.
Vander Beek, Doug, 52, 77, 165, 224, 226.
Vander Beek, Maryann, 226.
Vanderbush, Eric, 174.
Vanderbush, Fred, 18.
Vanderbush, Henry, 12.
Vanderbush, Ray, 18, 20.
Vander Plaats, Louis, 23-25.
Vander Pol, Bill, 184.
Vander Pol, Mike, 37.
Vander Pol, Myron, 49.
Vander Pol, Willy, 184.

Vanderstoep, Fred, 18.
Vanderstoop, Curt, 203, 204, 206, 208.
Van Essen, Barney, 51, 52, 54, 56, 72.
Van Essen, Larry, 184.
Van Hulzen, Bert, 46.
Van Nieuwenhuyzen, xi.
Van Ort, Delvie, 11.
Van Peursem, Jerry, 34.
Van Roekel, Bernard, 12.
Veenhof, Carla, 170.
Veenhof, Dean, x, xii, 20, 45, 46, 49-52, 54, 57, 58, 70, 71, 73, 74, 76, 78, 79, 80, 82, 84, 85, 87-90, 92, 96, 97, 99-101, 104, 105, 108, 110, 112-114, 115, 118, 119, 122, 128, 135, 138, 140, 141, 143, 147-149, 153, 154, 156, 158-162, 166, 170, 174, 176, 178, 181, 182, 185-191, 194, 198-200, 217, 218.
Veenhof, Judy, x, 218.
Veenhof, Nick, 34.
Veldhuizen, Eddie, 37.
Verdoes, Barb, 213.
Verdoes, Carol, 145, 170.
Verdoes, Dean, x, xii, xiii, 21, 46, 48, 50, 52, 54, 55, 57, 71-74, 76, 80, 82, 84, 87, 89, 92, 97-101. 104, 105, 108, 110, 111, 113, 115, 118, 126, 128, 138-142, 145, 148-150, 153, 154, 157-159, 161-163, 178, 181, 185, 186, 211, 213.
Verdoes, Francis, 90.
Verdoes, Gene, 145.
Verdoes, Harry, 145, 153.
Verdoom, Kathryn, 11.
Virginia, 8, 62, 64-66, 121, 122, 154, 205, 206.

EDGERTON

Visker, Lee, 88, 95.
Vlietstra, Nick, 171.
Vlietstra, Margaret, 171.
Vos, Ken, 184.
Voss, Lloyd, 54, 85, 89, 97, 172.
Vriesman, Pastor, 178.

Walhof, Ervin, 49.
Walnut Grove, 17, 95, 133.
Warn, Fred, 188, 189.
Warren, Cheryl, 221.
Warren, Tom, 21, 82, 83, 128, 186, 221.
Wassink, Darwin, 32, 33.
Wassink, Lloyd, 34, 36, 37.
Wassink, Pat, 156.
Wayzata, 79, 106, 128, 177.
Wells, 193, 194, 205, 206.
Werness, Bob, 130, 131.
Wensink, Gerrit "High Pockets," 28-30.
Wesselink, Harlen, 125.
Westbrook, 107.
Westenberg, Bob, 183, 186, 203-205.
Westenberg, Carroll, 37.
Westenberg, Duane, 29.
Westera, Hermina, 10.
Westera, Jeanette, 10.

Westergard, Robert, 23-26.
Westphal, Clark, 110.
Wiarda, Bob, x, xiii, 21, 49, 51, 52, 54, 70, 73, 81, 82, 92, 100, 110, 114, 119, 141, 149-151, 160-162, 180, 185, 186, 214.
Wilmont, 10.
Willmar, 7, 33, 131, 189.
Wilson, Gil, 69.
Windom, 143, 156, 172, 190.
Winona, 195, 197, 199.
Wolbrink, Adrian, 46.
Wolbrink, Dean, 165, 186.
Wolbrink, Reverend William G., 165.
Wood Lake, 96, 97.
Wooden, John, 73.
Woodstock, 16, 17, 26.
Worthington, 14, 15, 17, 24, 28, 29, 58, 90, 95, 96, 98, 103, 104, 107, 109, 112, 118, 125, 126, 152, 171, 172, 181, 185, 192-194, 212.

Youngsma, Allen, 18.

Zwart, Judy, 46, 145.
Zwart, Lloyd, 49, 45, 51, 52, 83.
Zylstra, John, 20.